Selected Sermons of John G. Lake

Volume 1 of 3

by John G. Lake

ISBN: 1539958876
ISBN-13: 978-1539958871

Copyright © 2016 Jawbone Digital
Yuma, Colorado

There is no education in faith like seeing God do the thing.
I have a conviction that you can pray and pray and pray until
Jesus comes, but unless you get up and believe Him for the thing
and commence to use what He has given you, you will never
know any more, and you really pray yourself into unbelief.
The results that God has given us demonstrate this to my mind.
—John G. Lake

A quick note from the publisher:

There is great value in the teachings of John G. Lake. If we didn't think so, you wouldn't be holding this book with our imprint stamped upon it.

Lake held to a controversial belief that taking medication or submitting yourself to the care of a doctor is sin. If you can live your life without medicine, wonderful! Lake attests that this is what an overcoming Christian life is supposed to look like, and expertly uses the Word of God to bolster his assertions.

However, you are responsible for your decisions, and Jawbone Digital holds no liability for what may or may not happen to you if you stop taking your medication.

Lake and others would likely call us cowardly for this disclaimer. I wonder what he would call those who face criminal charges for rejecting medical intervention while their children die?

Medication might not be God's ultimate plan, but neither is that.

TABLE OF CONTENTS

1

GOD'S WAY OF HEALING

God's way of healing is a person, not a thing. Jesus said. "I am the way, the truth, and the life." And He has ever been revealed to His people in all the ages by the Covenant Name, Jehovah Rophi, or, "I am the Lord that healeth thee," (John 14:6, Exodus 15:26)

The Lord Jesus Christ is still the healer. He can not change, for "He is the same yesterday, today, and forever," and He is still with us, for He said, "Lo, I am with you always, even unto the end of the world." (Hebrews 13:8, Matthew 28:20.) Because He is unchangeable, and because He is present, in Spirit, just as when in the flesh. He is the healer of His people.

Divine Healing rests on Christ's Atonement. It was prophesied of Him, "Surely He hath borne our grief, (Hebrew, sicknesses) and carried our sorrows, and with His stripes we are healed," and it is expressly declared that this was fulfilled in His ministry of Healing, which still continues. (Isaiah 53:4-5 Matthew 8:17)

Diseases can never be God's will. It is the Devil's work consequent on sin, and it is impossible for the work of the Devil ever to be the will of God. Christ came to destroy the works of the Devil and when He was on earth He, "healed every sickness and every disease," and all these diseases are expressly declared to have been the "oppression of the Devil." (1 John 3:8, Matthew 4:23, Acts 10:38.)

The gifts of Healing are permanent. It is expressly declared that the "gifts and callings of God are without repentance," and the Gifts of Healing are amongst the nine Gifts of the Spirit to the Church. (Romans 11:29, 1 Corinthians 12:8–11)

There are four modes of Divine Healing. The first is the direct prayer of faith: the second, intercessory prayer of two or more: the third, the anointing of the elders with the prayer of faith; and fourth, the laying on of hands by those who believe, and whom God has prepared and called to that ministry. (Matthew 8:5-13, Matthew 18:19, James 5:14-15, Mark 16:18.)

Multitudes have been healed through faith in Jesus. The writer knows of thousands of cases and has personally laid hands on scores of thousands of persons. Full information can be obtained at the meetings and Healing Rooms, 340 Rookery Bldg. Spokane, Washington. Also at the Masonic Temple meetings each Lord's day at 11 A.M. and 3 P.M. and in many pamphlets which give the experience, in their own words, of many who have been healed in this and other countries.

"Faith cometh by hearing, and hearing by the Word of God." You are heartily invited to attend and hear for yourself.

2

THE PLATFORM OF JESUS

There has always been a passage in the Declaration of Independence that has rung very deeply in my spirit. It was the thought of the Revolutionary Fathers in providing an explanation and reason to the world for undertaking to set up a new government among the families of nations. They said something like this: out of due respect for mankind they felt it necessary to give a reason for such an act.

As we invite this company of people together in this section of the country, I feel that a due word of loving explanation may be helpful.

I have been in this particular manner of ministry for many years. I believe Brother Fogwill and I began in this ministry some 16 or 17 years ago, or there about. Of course, we had been Christian ministers before that, but at that period God enlarged our vision of Himself and His purposes.

Personally, I received my ministry in the gospel of healing through John Alexander Dowie, a man whom I have loved with all my soul. And though in his later life he became broken in mind and committed many foolish things, so that discredit for a time was brought upon his work, I knew him from the beginning until the day of his death. I have gone to his grave since I have returned to this land, and as I have thought over that wonderful life, I have prayed in the silence of the night time, "Lord God endue me with the Spirit of God in the measure that you did that life."

I have always regarded it as a privilege in my life and as a unique thing, that after his death I was invited to preach in his pulpit, and I preached there for several months. I remember as I stood on the platform, above my head was a great crown possibly eight feet in diameter. It was made from boots with iron stirrups on them, thick soles, and all that character of thing that had come from people who had been healed of short limbs. Can you wonder, as I stood in that place, and looked around those walls, and saw plaster of Paris casts fastened on the walls, some of which had come off of my own friends who had been healed, iron braces that cripples had worn, cots on which the dying had been brought, one of them Anna Hicks. That cot was fastened to one of the walls above the gallery. And as I thought of the day when she was carried in practically dead, and that old man prayed for her and she was healed. And the company of her students who had lovingly escorted her to the station at Beren, Kentucky said to me, "We carried her as if we would if she had been dead, as pall bearers, and we received her back as from the dead."

Her friends cabled her and telegraphed her from all over the earth, and she gladly told the story, the wonderful story, almost the same character of story

4

that our Brother Zienke told you this morning, of the love of God, of the tenderness of the Christ that mankind has not known, of Jesus the Healer still.

Beloved, there is a deep passionate yearning in my soul, that above all else, this congregation may set forth to the praise of God such a character of righteousness in God, such a purity of holiness from God, that this people may not only be recognized in this city, but throughout the world, as a people among whom God dwells.

Beginning this work, as I do at this time, I want to say that I do not come as a novice to this time of my life. God has permitted me in the years that are past to assist in the establishment of two great works of God, each of them on a new plane in God. I trust, blessed be His Name, that in calling together once again the people of God, that it shall be to establish a work on a new plane. Indeed, a higher one that our souls have ever known, where the radiant purity of the holiness of God shall be shed forth into the whole world. And I believe that is God's purpose.

Jesus, Himself, stood at Nazareth on an almost similar occasion. He had been raised in one of the country towns. He had disappeared from His community, gone down to the Jordan, and had been baptized of John. The Holy Ghost had come upon Him, and He had returned to his own home town, to the synagogue where He had worshipped as a boy.

One thing I have always praised God for is that when God put me into public ministry, He made me start in the very town, the very community, next door to the very home where I had been raised. When a man fights out the battles of life in his own community, in his own home town, among his friends and neighbors, and receives love and confidence from them, I always feel he has received a good preparation for the next step in life. Jesus knew the place for a man to begin to serve God when He had said to the demoniac of Gadara who was delivered, "Go home to thy friends, and show them how great things the Lord hath done for thee" (Mark 5:19).

If your wife does not know you are a Christian nobody else will be likely to. If your husband does not know you are a Christian, it is a poor testimony. It is the woman that is with you, who eats with you, and sleeps with you, that will know whether you are a child of God or not. It is the man who lives in the same house with you, and the people in your community, who will know best how much of the life of God radiates from your own soul.

So Jesus stood in His own home town of Nazareth and read this wonderful text that I am going to read this morning. It is known, or ought to be, as the platform of Jesus Christ.

"The Spirit of the Lord is upon me, because he hath anointed me to preach the gospel to the poor."

THE POOR. (Jesus Christ has an anti-poverty program) That is the first duty of every child of God and every Church of God that ever came into existence. And the Church that fails in that duty to mankind has failed in the first principle, and has denied the first principle of the platform of the Son of God.

My heart has never gone out in sympathy to a body of Christian people who became a little clique and represent a certain select number of society. My conception of the real Church of God is one where rich and poor alike, bless God, feel at home, where there are no barriers and no boundaries but where soul flows out to soul, and in the larger life man knows only man and God. Blessed be His precious Name.

"The Spirit of the Lord is upon me, because he hath anointed me to preach the gospel to the poor."

The ministry of the things of God must ever be without money and without price. My soul could never descend to the place where charges are made for the services of the minister of the gospel of Christ. Never, Bless God!

It is our privilege to make possible a ministry to the people without money and without price, bless God. The magnanimity of the Lord Jesus Christ has stood out as blessed and wonderful feature in all His ministry. I have sometimes wondered how many people really knew how the Lord existed during His own earth life. The Word of God gives us one little hint in these words: "Joanna, the wife of Chuza, Herod's steward, and Susanna, and many others, which ministered unto him of their substance." That was how the Son of God was able to minister without money and without price to mankind. We today have that privilege too. It is ours. I have faith in God that this Church will demonstrate Christ's ministry to the poor.

For ten years God has privileged me to preach the gospel without salary, without collections. I never asked a man for a cent in my life, and I have lived, bless God, and been able to minister every day. God has met me every time, and I believe He will meet every other man and woman who will likewise put their trust in God and go forward.

The second plank in the platform of the Gospel of Jesus Christ is this:

"To heal the broken hearted."

There are lots of them. I tell you since I have been in Spokane the Lord has let me into the homes of the rich and poor, and it is not in the poor districts that you find all the broken hearted by any means. "He hath sent Me to heal the broken hearted," that is the ministry of this body. If there is a broken hearted soul in your locality, you are the one, who in the Name of Jesus Christ, has the privilege of ministering in the things of God to that soul: broken hearted because of sin, broken hearted, sometimes by sickness, broken hearted because of the conditions around them that they seem unable to control.

When I see the living God in His tender mercy touch one and another and make them whole, whether in spirit, in soul, or in body, I rejoice equally in either case, for what God does is always good, and worthy of praise. I regard the healing of a man's body to be just as sacred as the healing of his soul. There is no distinction, Jesus made none. He provided a perfect salvation for mankind: all that man needed for spirit, soul or body.

So this ministry, bless God, will be a healing ministry. This Church will be a healing Church. This will be a Church to which you can invite your friends who are ill, and bring them here, and help them. I trust after a time we will be able to bring the people in great numbers, the sick who are on cots and stretchers and crutches, that the Lord Jesus through this Church and its ministry may make them well.

It is my purpose that a number of brethren, who have had this same burden on their hearts for many years as I have had it, may come together in this city as a Headquarters, and that from this city we may extend this ministry throughout the land. I have particularly invited my old preaching partner, Brother Cyrus B. Fockler, of Milwaukee, my dear, precious brother, Archibald Fairley, of Zion City, a prophet of God and one of the anointed of the Lord, Brother Bert Rice of Chicago, my dear Brother Charles W. Westwood, of Portland, Oregon, and Reverend

Fogwell to assist me in this ministry. Brother Westwood visited with me a few days, and is now going on to Chicago to make the necessary arrangements.

This is the outline so far as God has made it clear. This is to be a healing Church. Everyone who has been called to this ministry and those who will be called in the future will minister to body and soul and spirit through the Lord Jesus Christ.

The third plank in the platform of Jesus Christ is this:

"To preach deliverance to the captives."

How many there are! One day, not long ago, I received a telephone call from a lady in one of the Missions saying that she had a man there who was a terrible drunkard. Every once in a while he would get delirium tremens. He saw devils: he was haunted by them. The lady said, "We can not do anything for him. We thought perhaps you could help him." He came up to see me. He sat down to tell me about himself. Right away I could discern that he was a soul who from his very birth had been gifted with spiritual sight. But instead of associating in the spirit with angels, with God, with Christ, all his spiritual association was with devils, demons, horrors, until that to escape from that condition he had become a drunk in his youth. In order to have relaxation for a time, he had paralyzed himself with drink, and that was his difficulty.

I said to him, "my son, kneel down. We are going to pray to God." And I prayed that God would bind every last demon and lift his soul into union with God, and fill him with the Holy Ghost, so he might associate with the angels of God and become a new man in Christ, and have fellowship with the Holy Spirit.

In a few days he returned and said, "Oh, brother, it is all so new, so different. As I walk along the street there are no more demons, no more devils; but as I came up to the Church today an angel, so beautiful, so sweet, so pure, walked by my side. And, Brother, there he is now, and He has wounds on His hands and on His feet." But my eyes were dim; I could not see Him. I presume they were like the eyes of the servant of Elisha. "To preach deliverance to the captives" from all kinds of powers, earthly and sensual. It is the privilege of the real Church to bring deliverance to the captives of sin, of disease, of death and hell, not only proclaim the message of deliverance but exercise the power of God to set them free.

The fourth plank:

"Recovering of sight to the blind."

Among the blessed healings of the past few weeks is one dear soul who is not yet completely healed, a blind woman whose eyes have gradually opened day by day from the first morning of prayer, and who will be present with us in the near future, as Brother Zeinke was this morning, to praise God for her deliverance.

"Recovering of sight to the blind." But there are many blind hearts, blind minds, blind souls, just as well as blind eyes, who do not see the beauty and power of the things of Christ. And to them we bring today the message of our Christ, "recovering of sight to the blind."

I pray above every other thing this Church will be a Church that will know God so intimately that when men come in contact with any one of us they will feel that they have met one who is able to reveal the Lord Jesus Christ to them. I believe it will be so.

The fifth plank:

"To set at liberty them that are bruised."

There are the bleeding ones, the bruised ones, those who have been hid away, and those whose life has been made a burden. May I tell you this incident.

The last night I preached in my tabernacle in Johannesburg, they brought a young man with whom life had gone so very hard. He had lost hope and had gone into despair so that he tried to blot himself out by committing suicide. He shot himself in the mouth, and the bullet came out the back of the head, strangely without killing him. This left him with a violent pain in the base of the brain that caused him to suffer untold agony, and his neck was rigid.

This night the greatest part of the congregation was composed of Cornish miners, whom I have regarded as the hardest men I have ever met in South Africa. They live a very hard, terrible life. They dissipate terribly.

This man came up on the platform to be prayed for, and I wanted the sympathy of the people. So I made a plea in some such words as these: "Here is a poor fellow with whom life has gone so hard that he tried to blot himself out, and in his endeavor to do so, he shot himself, with the result that he is in the condition you see him in now." Presently I began to observe that up from the audience there came a wave of loving sympathy. I said, "If you never prayed in your life, if you never prayed for yourself, bow your head and pray tonight and ask God to deliver your fellow man."

I put my hands on him and prayed, and the power of God came down upon him and instantly the joints became loose, the neck pliable, the pain gone. Looking up into my face, he said, "Who did that?" I said, "That was the Lord Jesus Christ." And dropping on his knees before me he said, "Brother, show me how to find that Christ; I want to know Him."

Down in the audience that night was one of the most cultured gentlemen it has ever been my privilege to know. He raised in his seat and reverently raising his hands, he said, "My Lord and my God." He had not been a Christian, but he saw a new vision of the love of God for man that night.

Away back in the audience another soul was touched. He was a different type of man. He came from a different environment. He raised up and slapped himself on the hip, and shouted, "Bully for Jesus!" It came out of the depth of his soul.

Beloved, it is my conviction that the purity of Jesus Christ and the radiant holiness and the power of God will manifest Christ alike to the cultured and the uncultured, for both hearts are hungry when they see the living Christ.

The sixth plank of the platform:

"To preach the acceptable year of the Lord."

Not next year, not in five years, not when you die, but a present salvation, a present healing for spirit, soul and body. Blessed be His Name. All you need, bless God, is to bring your whole being into perfect harmony with the living God so that the Spirit of God radiates through your spirit, radiates through your mind, and radiates likewise through your body. Blessed be His Name.

Among the most precious privileges that is given to the real Church is to be in fact, not in word alone, the Body of Christ. The Word of God speaks of "The Church," which is His body. And as God, the Father, manifested Himself through that one beautiful, holy, purified body of Jesus Christ in such a perfect manner, when men looked upon Him they did not see the man Jesus, but they saw God. Then He

14

ascended and sent the Holy Spirit to the Church, to you and to me. What for? That the new Body should come forth, and the Church, the real Church, united to God and filled with the Holy Ghost, should manifest God again to mankind through this Body. That Church is made up of all that are written in the Lamb's Book of Life.

When God wants to heal a man, the healing does not fall down from heaven, but it does come through the medium of the child of God. Therefore, God has given us the exalted privilege of being co-laborers together with God. And among our high privileges is to radiate, to give forth from the love passion of our souls the courage and strength to help other souls to come to God. And the business of the Church is to be a savior, or saviors, for the Word of God says, "And saviors shall come up on Mount Zion." These are those in such union with God that they are able to lift mankind up to the "Lamb of God that taketh away the sin of the world."

3

THE BAPTISM OF THE HOLY GHOST: PART 1

The Baptism of the Holy Ghost is a most difficult subject to discuss with any degree of intelligence, for though we may not care to admit it, the fact remains that the density of ignorance among the people, and the ministry, on this subject is appalling. To view this subject with any degree of intelligence we must view it from the standpoint of progressive revelation. Like Christian baptism, the operation of the Holy Ghost must be seen (comprehended) in its various stages of revelation. Otherwise we shall be unable to distinguish between the operations of the Spirit in the Old Testament dispensation and the Baptism of the Holy Ghost in the New Testament.

As we approach the threshold of this subject it seems as if the Spirit of God comes close to us. A certain awe of God comes over the soul. And it is my earnest wish that no levity, satire, or sarcasm be permitted to enter into this discussion. Such things would be grievous to the tender Spirit of God.

In the beginning of this revelation after the deluge, it seems as if God was approaching man from a great distance, so far had sin removed man from his original union with God at the time of his creation. God seems to reveal Himself to man as rapidly as man by progressive stages of development is prepared to receive the revelation. Consequently we see that the Baptism was a further revelation of God's purpose in purifying the heart from sin than was the original ceremony of circumcision; so the Baptism of the Holy Ghost is a greater, more perfect revelation of God than were the manifestations of the Spirit in the Patriarchal or Mosaic dispensations.

Three distinct dispensations of God are clearly seen, each with an ever-deepening manifestation of God to man. A preceding dispensation of God never destroys a foregoing richer revelation of God. This is manifestly seen in looking at the Patriarchal, Mosaic, and Christian dispensations. In the Patriarchal dispensation we see God appearing to man at long intervals. Abraham furnishes the best example, for to him God appeared at long intervals of 20 and 40 years apart; so with the other patriarchs. Under the Mosaic dispensation there is a deeper and clearer manifestation of God. God was ever-present in the pillar of cloud and the pillar of fire. He was present also in the tabernacle where the Shekinah Glory overshadowed the Mercy Seat. This is a continuous, abiding revelation of God. It was God with man not to man as was the Patriarchal dispensation. God was leading, guiding, directing, forgiving, sanctifying and abiding with man. But the revelation of God under the Christian Dispensation is a much deeper and truer revelation of God than this. It is God in man. It is the actual incoming of the Spirit of God to live in man.

This brings us then to where we can see the purpose of God in revealing Himself to man in progressive steps of revelations.

Man by progressive stages through repentance and faith is purified, not alone forgiven his transgressions, but cleansed from the nature of sin within that causes him to transgress. This cleansing from inbred sin, the nature of sin, the carnal mind, the old Man, and so on, is the actual taking out of our breast the desire for sin, and all correspondence with sin in us is severed. The carnal life is laid a sacrifice on the altar of Christ in glad surrender by us. This inner heart cleansing that John and the disciples of Christ demanded is the work of the Holy Spirit by the blood and is necessary if maturity in Christ is to be achieved. A holy God must have a holy dwelling place. Oh wondrous salvation, wondrous Christ, wondrous atonement, man born in sin, shaped in iniquity, forgiven, cleansed, purified outside and inside by the blood of Jesus and made a habitation of God. It was that man once created in the likeness of God should again become the dwelling place of God. That is what the atoning blood of Christ provided (Galatians 3:13-14). Christ hath redeemed us from the curse of the law, being made a curse for us; for it is written, "Cursed is every one that hangeth on a tree," that the blessing of Abraham might come on the Gentiles through Jesus Christ that they might receive the promise of the Spirit through faith. This reveals to us God's purpose by the blood of Jesus Christ for us now to become the habitation of God: "In whom ye also are builded together for a habitation of God through the Spirit" (Ephesians 2:22). Again in 1 Corinthians 6:19, we see Paul in astonishment saying, "What? Know ye not that your body is the temple of the Holy Ghost?" Let us now see where we are and we will better understand how to go on.

The Holy Ghost is the Spirit of God. His purpose is to dwell in man after man's perfect cleansing from sin through the blood of Jesus Christ. His coming was definite, just as definite as was the advent of Jesus. When Jesus was born, his birth was proclaimed by an angel voice and chanted by a multitude of the heavenly host praising God (Luke 2:9-14.) Equally so was the Holy Spirit's advent attested by His bodily form as a dove (Luke 3:22), and by His sound from heaven as of a rushing mighty wind and by cloven tongues of fire upon each of them (Acts 2:2-3). Heavenly dove, tempest roar, and tongues of fire crowning the hundred and twenty were as convincing as the guiding star and midnight shout of angel hosts. The coming of the Holy Ghost upon the hundred and twenty is found in Acts 2.

At the Last Supper when Jesus addressed the disciples, He said to them, "Nevertheless I tell you the truth; it is expedient for you that I go away: for if I go not away, the Comforter will not come unto you; but if I depart, I will send Him unto you. And when He is come, He will reprove the world of sin, and of righteousness, and of judgment" (John 16:7-8). As the disciples were together at Jerusalem after the resurrection, when the two who had walked with him to Emmaus were conversing with the eleven disciples, Jesus Himself stood in their midst. He said unto them, "Peace be unto you." They were affrighted, believing they had seen a spirit. Jesus addressed them and said, "And, behold, I send the promise of the Father upon you: but tarry ye in the city of Jerusalem until ye be endued with power from on high" (Luke 24:49). Then in Acts 1, we find that the one hundred and twenty tarried in prayer in the upper room ten days. Thus between the crucifixion of Jesus and Pentecost is 53 days.

There was a crucifixion day. It was necessary. And now, we the children of God, must be crucified with Christ and freed from sin, our old man nailed to the cross. We die to sin, a real act, a genuine experience; it is done. So we are made partakers of Christ's death. But there was a resurrection day. He arose as a living Christ, not a dead one. He livest! He lives! And by our resurrection with Him into our new life, we leave the old sin life and the old man buried in baptism (Romans 6), and are made partakers of His new resurrection life. The life of power, the exercise of the power of God, is made possible to us by Jesus having elevated us into His own resurrection life by actual spiritual experience.

Then comes His ascension, just as necessary as the crucifixion or the resurrection. Jesus ascends to heaven and sits triumphant at the right hand of the

Father. And according to His promise, He sent upon us the Holy Ghost. This experience is personal and dispensational. The Holy Ghost descends upon us, entering into us, for the Baptism of the Holy Ghost is the Holy God, the Spirit of Jesus, taking possession of our personality, living in us, moving us, controlling us. We become partakers of His glorified life, the life of Christ in glory. So it was with the hundred and twenty (see Acts 2:2-4): "And suddenly there came a sound from heaven as of a rushing mighty wind." (Suppose we heard it now. What would the audience think?) "And it filled all the house where they were sitting. And there appeared unto them cloven tongues like as of fire and it sat upon each of them. And they were all filled with the Holy Ghost, and began to speak in other tongues, as the Spirit gave them utterance." It was the Spirit that spoke in other tongues. What spirit? The Holy Ghost who had come into them, who controlled them, who spoke through them. Listen! Speaking in tongues is the voice of God. Do you hear God's voice? They spake as the Spirit gave them utterance.

Now we have advanced to where we can understand God's manifestations. Not God witnessing to man. Not God with man, But God in man. They spake as the Spirit gave them utterance.

At this point the Spirit of God fell on Brother Lake causing him to speak in tongues in an unknown language. The audience was asked to bow their heads

21

in silent prayer for the interpretation of the words spoken in tongues. As they prayed the interpretation was given as follows:

"Christ is at once the spotless descent of God into man and the sinless ascent of man into God. And the Holy Spirit is the agent by which it is accomplished."

He is the Christ, the Son of God. His atonement is a real atonement. It changes from all sin. Man again becomes the dwelling place of God. Let us now see one of the most miraculous chapters in all the Word of God, Acts 10. A man, Cornelius, is praying. He is a Gentile centurion. An angel appears to him. The angel speaks. The angel says to send to Joppa for Peter. Peter is a Jew and he is not supposed to go into the home of a Gentile. He has not learned that salvation is for the Gentiles. God has to teach him. How does God do it? Peter goes up on the housetop to pray, and as he prays he is in a trance. Think of it! A trance. He falls into a trance. Suppose I was to fall on the floor in a trance: nine-tenths of this audience would be frightened to death. They would instantly declare that my opponent had hypnotized me. Why? Because of the ignorance among men of how the Spirit of God operates. But listen, listen! As he lays on the roof in a trance he sees a vision, a sheet let down from heaven caught by the four corners full of all manner of beasts and creeping things. And a voice —what voice?—the Lord's voice said, "Rise, Peter, kill and eat." But Peter said, "Not so, Lord. I have

22

never eaten anything common or unclean." But the Voice said, "What I have cleansed that call thou not common." Peter obeyed. He went with the messengers. Now see the result. As he spake the Word "the Holy Ghost fell on all them that heard the word. And they of the circumcision which believed were astonished, as many as came with Peter, because that on the Gentiles also was poured out the Holy Ghost." How did they know? "They heard them speak with tongues and magnify God." Then answered Peter, "Can any man forbid water that these should not be baptized which have received the Holy Ghost as well as we?" And so it all ended in a glorious baptismal service in water of all who had been baptized in the Holy Ghost.

In Acts 22:12, Paul tells of Ananias coming to see him, but how did Ananias know Paul was there? See Acts 9:10-19. "And there was at Damascus a certain disciple named Ananias and to him the Lord said in a vision, go into the street called Straight and inquire at the house of Judas for one called Saul of Tarsus." Now let us see that as we would see it today. The Lord said, "Ananias, go down into Straight Street to the house of Judas and ask for a man named Saul of Tarsus for behold he prayeth." And now the Lord tells Ananias what Saul had seen (Acts 9:12): "and hath seen in a vision a man named Ananias coming in and putting his hands on him that he might receive his sight." Here Ananias talks with the Lord. Do you know anything of such communion or talks with

God? If not, get the Baptism of the Holy Ghost like the early Christians, and their knowledge and experiences afterward can be yours, and you will see as we do the operation of the Lord upon saint and sinner by the Holy Ghost. Men say to us, "Where do you men get your insight into the Word?" We get it just where Paul and Peter got it: from God by the Holy Ghost. (Galatians 1:11-12)

Beloved, read God's Word on your knees. Ask God by His Spirit to open it to your understanding. Read the Word with an open heart. It is a lamp unto our feet and a light unto our path.

Ananias went as the Lord had directed him and found Paul. And Paul was healed of his blindness and was baptized in the Holy Ghost and was also baptized in water and spoke in tongues "more than ye all." (1 Corinthians 14:18)

Now see again Acts 22:14. Ananias is speaking to Paul, and he said, "The God of our Fathers hath chosen thee, that thou shouldst know his will, and see that Just One, and shouldst hear the words of his mouth. For thou shall be his witness unto all men of what thou hast seen and heard." Say, what about the people who say, "Don't tell these things to anyone." "And now why tarriest thou? Arise, and be baptized, and wash away thy sins calling upon the name of the Lord." You see, as with Peter at Cornelius' house, all this work of the Spirit ended in salvation and baptism.

Now God through Ananias promised Paul that he

should know "His will and see that Just One and shouldest hear the voice of his mouth," (Acts 22:14). When did that come to pass? Three years after when Paul returned to Jerusalem. "Then after three years I went up to Jerusalem," (Galatians 1:18). "And it came to pass that when I was come again to Jerusalem, even while I prayed in the temple, I was in a trance," (Acts 22:17). Think of it, the intellectual, wonderful Paul, the master theologian of the ages, the orator of orators, the logician of logicians in a trance. Bless God for that trance. It was the fulfillment of what Ananias had said to him three years before. "And saw him (Jesus) saying unto me, Make haste and get thee quickly out of Jerusalem for they will not receive thy testimony concerning me." Now what is a trance? A trance is the Spirit taking predominance over the mind and body, and for the time being, the control of the individual is by the Spirit; but our ignorance of the operations of God is such that even ministers of religion have been known to say it is the devil.

Let us see where Paul got his commission to preach and instructions about what he was to preach, and what his condition and attitude were when Jesus gave him his commission.

See Acts 26:16-18. He was lying on the road on his way to Damascus. Now if we were to see someone lying on the road talking to an invisible somebody, no doubt in our ignorance we would send for an ambulance or for the police. But this is where the glorified Christ spoke to Paul and gave him definite instructions about what he should preach; and the purpose of his preaching was to be the salvation, not the entertainment, of others. "But rise, stand upon thy feet: for I (Jesus) have appeared unto thee for this purpose, to make thee a minister and a witness both of these things which thou hast seen, and of those things in the which I will appear unto thee." Jesus promises to appear to Paul again, and that was fulfilled while he lay in a trance in the temple three years later (Acts 26:16).

Now the object of his preaching was "to open their eyes, and to turn them from darkness to light, and from the power of Satan unto God, that they may receive forgiveness of sins, and inheritance among them which are sanctified (present experience) by faith that is in me (Jesus). Whereupon, O King Agrippa, I was not disobedient unto the heavenly vision" (Acts 26:18-19).

From this we see and are able to understand the operations of God by His Spirit. And now, is the Holy Ghost in the Church today? Verily, yes; but you say, "We do not see Him work in this way. Why is it?" Because you say all these things were for the Apostolic days. You can not take the Word of God and find one place where the gifts of the Holy Ghost were withdrawn.

The nine gifts of the Holy Ghost are found in 1 Corinthians 12:8-11: "For to one is given by the Spirit the word of wisdom, to another the word of knowledge by the same Spirit, to another discerning of spirits, to another divers (different) kinds of tongues (languages) (not an acquirement but by the Spirit), to another faith by the same Spirit, to another gifts of healing by the same Spirit." Oh, praise God for the discovery of the gifts of the Holy Ghost and especially for the gift of healing. May we all learn to know Christ not alone as our Savior but as our sanctifier and healer, too.

Now I will go over these gifts on my fingers: 1st, wisdom; 2nd, knowledge; 3rd, faith; 4th, healing; 5th, miracles; 6th, prophecy; 7th, discerning of spirits; 8th, divers kinds of tongues; and 9th, the interpretation of tongues. We have seen that the Holy Ghost came into the Church at Pentecost and the gifts are in the Holy Ghost; consequently, if the Holy Ghost is in the Church, the gifts are, too. Because of the lack of faith we do not see them exercised in the ordinary Church. We stand for the obtaining of the gifts of the Holy Ghost through our personal baptism in the Holy Ghost and the enduement of the Holy Ghost power as promised by Jesus, yea, commanded by Him in Acts 1:8: "Ye shall receive power after that the Holy Ghost is come upon you…"

People ask, "What is tongues?" Tongues is the voice (or operation) of the Spirit of God within. When the Holy Ghost came in He spoke, Again, in Acts 10:44-48, when the Holy Ghost fell on them, Peter demanded the right to baptize them in water, saying, "Can any man forbid water, that these would be baptized, which have received the Holy Ghost?" See verse 46, "for they heard them speak with tongues, and magnify God." Tongues is the evidence of the baptism of the Holy Ghost by which Peter claimed the right to baptize them in water. Again in Acts 19:1-7, Paul at Ephesus met twelve men whom John had baptized unto repentance, but now Paul re-baptized them by Christian Baptism. In verse 5 we read that when they heard this, they were baptized (water baptism) in the Name of the Lord Jesus. And when Paul had laid his hands on them, the Holy Ghost came on them and they spoke with tongues and prophesied. "Tongues are for a sign, not to them that believe, but to them that believe not." (1 Corinthians 14:22)

4

THE BAPTISM OF THE HOLY GHOST: PART 2

There are as many degrees in God in the Baptism of the Holy Ghost as there are preachers who preach it. Some people are born away down weeping at the foot of the cross. They are still on the earth plane with Christ. They are still weeping over their sins, still trying to overcome sin and be pure of heart.

But there are other people who are born away up in the blessed dominion of God, like our Mother Etter. They have resurrection power. All power is given, and it is in our soul.

And beloved, one day there are going to be Christians, baptized in the Holy Ghost who are away up in the Throne of God, away up in the consciousness that is breathed out of His holy heart. Somebody is going to be born a son of God; and be baptized in the Holy Ghost where Jesus is today, in the Throne-consciousness of Christ. Where they can say, like Jesus said, where they can feel like Jesus feels: "I am He that liveth, and was dead, and behold. I am alive for evermore and have the keys of hell and of death." Absolute overcoming consciousness!

You dear folks listen, who are trying to pump up a Pentecost that has worn out years ago. God let it die.

God had only one way under heaven to get you to move up into God, and that way is to let you become dissatisfied with the thing you have. And if you have not the consciousness you once had, God Almighty understands the situation. He is trying to get you hungry so that you will commit your Body and your Soul and your Spirit to God forever, and by the grace of God you will be baptized in the Holy Ghost over again, at the Throne of God-consciousness, in the power of Jesus Christ., as Jesus is today. "As He is, so are we in this world."

Why, with most of you, when you were baptized in the Holy Ghost the Lord had to baptize a whole dose of medicine, and pills, and everything that was in you. Well, God never had to baptize that kind of stuff in the Lord Jesus. Jesus came down to the River Jordan, and gave His BODY and His SOUL and His SPIRIT to God forever, and He never took a pill or a dose of medicine. He never went to the spirit of the world for assistance: or to the devil for help. His SPIRIT, His SOUL, and His BODY were God's from that minute, forever.

Beloved, God is calling men and women to a holier consecration, to a higher place in God, and I am one of God's candidates for that holy place in God. I want to get to the Throne of God. Oh, yes, God baptized me in the Holy Ghost with a wondrous baptism, according to the understanding I possessed ten or fifteen years ago. But I am a candidate today for a new baptism in the Holy Ghost that comes out of the heart of the GLORIFIED Christ, in the lightnings of God; everlasting overcoming; on the throne with Jesus.

And that is the experience that is going to make the sons of God in the world. That is the reason they will take the world for Jesus Christ, and the Kingdom will be established, and they will put the crown on the Son of God and declare Him "King of kings and Lord of lords" forever. Amen.

Therefore, fear not., for God is able to perform in you even that which He performed in Jesus, and raise you likewise in union with Christ Jesus, and make you reign in dominion over sin, instead of being dominated by the powers of evil and darkness.

Message given through tongues and interpretation in Battle Creek, Michigan, September, 1913.

5

THE BAPTISM OF THE HOLY GHOST: PART 3

The Baptism of the Holy Ghost was of such importance in the mind of the Lord Jesus Christ that He commanded His disciples to tarry in Jerusalem "until ye be endued with power from on high" (Acts 1:8). And they steadfastly carried out what the Lord had commanded, waiting on God in a continuous prayer meeting in the upper room for ten days until the Promise of the Father was fulfilled (Luke 24:49), and that Baptism had fallen of which John the Baptist spoke in Matthew 3:11, saying, "I indeed baptize you with water unto repentance, but He that cometh after me is mightier than I, whose shoes I am not worthy to bear: He shall baptize you with the Holy Ghost and with fire."

In order to obtain from Heaven the Spirit of Jesus (the Holy Ghost), it is first necessary that the individual shall know that his sins are blotted out, that the blood of Jesus Christ has sanctified his heart and cleansed him from the sinful nature, or the Adamic nature, the inherent nature of sin (Ephesians 2:1-3).

Personally I knew that my sins had been blotted out, but it was only two months prior to my Baptism in the Holy Ghost that I learned by the Word of God

32

and experienced in my life the sanctifying power of God subduing the soul and cleansing the nature from sin. This inward life cleansing was to me the crowning work of God in my life at that period, and I shall never cease to praise God that He revealed to me the depth by the Holy Ghost the power of the blood of Jesus.

Many inquire what is the reason that when your heart is sanctified and the conscious knowledge of your cleansing has taken place that you are not instantly baptized with the Holy Ghost. From my own experience and the experiences of others it is readily seen that, notwithstanding that the heart is cleansed from sin, it is still necessary in many instances for the dear Lord to further spiritualize the personality until the individual has become sufficiently receptive to receive within his person the Holy Ghost. The forces of our personality must be subdued unto God. This we commonly speak of as spiritualizing. In many instances even though the heart is really pure, yet the individual has not at once received the Baptism of the Holy Ghost, and in some instances has given up in despair and turned back to his first works, believing that there must still be sin in his heart, thus discrediting what God has already done within him through the blood of Jesus. No, it is not always that the heart is still impure. It is not because you are not thoroughly sanctified. It is only God waiting and working to bring you to the place and to sufficiently spiritualize your personality that you may receive into your being the Holy Ghost.

The Baptism of the Holy Ghost is not an influence, nor yet a good feeling, nor sweet sensations, though it may include all of these. The Baptism of the Holy Ghost is the incoming into the personality of Him, the Holy Ghost, which is the Spirit of Jesus taking real possession of your spirit (or inner man), of your soul (the mind and animal life), yea, of your flesh. He possesses the being. The flesh is caused to quake sometimes because of the presence of the Spirit of God in the flesh. Daniel quaked with great quaking when the Spirit of the Lord came upon him (Daniel 10:1-13).

Beloved reader, do you realize that it is the Spirit of Jesus that is seeking admittance into your heart and life? Do you realize that it is the Spirit of Jesus within the spirit, soul and body of the baptized believer that moves him in ways sometimes strange, but who accomplishes the wondrous work of God within the life that every baptized believer praises God has taken place in him?

While yet a justified man, even without an experience of sanctification, the Lord committed to me in a measure the ministry of healing inasmuch that many were healed, and, in some instances, real miracles of healing took place. Yet I did not know God as my sanctifier. Ten years later, after sanctification had become a fact in my life, a great and wonderful yearning to be baptized in the Holy Ghost and fire came into my heart. After seeking God persistently, almost night and day for two months, the Lord baptized me in the Holy Ghost causing me to speak in tongues and magnify God. I had looked for and prayed and coveted the real power of God for the ministry of healing and believed God that when I was baptized in the Holy Ghost that His presence in me through the Spirit would do for the sick the things my heart desired and which they needed. Instantly upon being baptized in the Spirit I expected to see the sick healed in a greater degree and in larger numbers than I had before known, and, for a times I seemed to be disappointed.

How little we know of our own relationship to God! How little I knew of my own relationship to Him; for, day by day, for six months following my Baptism in the Holy Ghost the Lord revealed to me many things in my life where repentance, confession and restitution were necessary, and yet I had repented unto God long ago. O, the deep cleansings, the deep revelations of one's own heart by the Holy Ghost. It was indeed as John the Baptist said, "whose fan is in his hand, and he will thoroughly purge his floor, and gather his wheat into the garner: but the chaff he will burn up with unquenchable fire."

First, then, I will say the Baptism in the Holy Ghost meant to me a heart searching as I have never before known, with no rest, until in every instance the blood was consciously applied, and my life set free from the particular thing that God had revealed. As I say, this process continued for six months after my

Baptism in the Holy Spirit.

Second, a love for mankind such as I had never comprehended took possession of my life. Yea, a soul yearning to see men saved, so deep, at times heart rending, until in anguish of soul I was compelled to abandon my business and turn all my attention to bringing men to the feet of Jesus. While this process was going on in my heart, during a period of months, sometimes persons would come to my office to transact business and even instances where there were great profits to be had for a few minutes of persistent application to business, the Spirit of love in me so yearned over souls that I could not even see the profits to be had. Under its sway, money lost its value to me and in many instances I found myself utterly unable to talk business to the individual until first I had poured out the love passion of my soul and endeavored to show him Jesus as his then present Savior. In not just a few instances these business engagements ended in the individual yielding himself to God.

That love passion for men's souls has sometimes been overshadowed by the weight of care since then, but only for a moment. Again, when occasion demanded it, that mighty love flame absorbing one's whole being and life would flame forth until, under the anointing of the Holy Ghost on many occasions sinners would fall in my arms and yield their hearts to God.

Others have sought for evidences of this

Pentecostal experience being the real baptism of the Holy Ghost. Some have criticized and said, "Is it not a delusion?" In all the scale of evidences presented to my soul and taken from my experience, this experience of the divine love, the burning love and holy compassion of Jesus Christ filling one's bosom until no sacrifice is too great to win a soul for Christ demonstrates to me more than any other one thing that this is indeed none other than the Spirit of Jesus. Such love is not human! Such love is only divine! Such love is only Jesus Himself, who gave His life for others.

Again, the development of power. First, after the mighty love came the renewed, energized power for healing of the sick. O what blessed things God has given on this line! What glorious resurrections of the practically dead! Such restorations of the lame and the halt and the blind! Such shouts of joy! Such abundance of peace! Verily, "Himself took our infirmities and bare our sicknesses."

Then came as never before the power to preach the Word of God in demonstration of the Spirit. O, the burning fiery messages; O, the tender, tender, loving messages! Oh, the deep revelations of wondrous truth by the Holy Ghost! Preaching once, twice, sometimes three times a day, practically continuously during these four years and four months. O, the thousands God has permitted us to lead to the feet of Jesus, and the tens of thousands to whom He has permitted us to preach the Word!

Then came the strong, forceful exercise of dominion over devils, to cast them out. Since that time many insane and demon possessed, spirits of insanity, all sorts of unclean demons, have been cast out in the mighty name of Jesus through the power of the precious blood. Saints have been led into deeper life in God. Many, many have been baptized in the Holy Ghost and fire. My own ministry was multiplied a hundredfold in the very lives of others to whom God committed this same ministry. Yea, verily the Baptism in the Holy Ghost is to be desired with the whole heart.

Brother, Sister, when we stand before the bar of God and are asked why we have not fulfilled in our life all the mind of Christ and all His desire in the salvation of the world, how will be our excuses if they are weighed against the salvation of imperishable souls? How terrible it will be for us to say we neglected, we put off, we failed to seek for the enduement that cometh from on high, the Baptism of the Holy Ghost.

Again, are we close, may we say that it was only after the Lord had baptized us in the Holy Ghost that we really learned how to pray? When He prayed through us, when the soul cries born of the Holy Ghost rolled out of your being and up to the throne of God, the answer came back: His prayer, His heart yearning, His cry. May God put it in every heart that we may indeed see the answer to our Lord's prayer, "Thy Kingdom come; Thy will be done on earth as it is done in Heaven."

But someone will say, "How about tongues? We understood that you taught that tongues were the evidence of the Baptism in the Holy Ghost?" So they are. "Tongues are a sign to them that believe not." (1 Corinthians 14:22) While I personally praise God for the wonderful and blessed truths of His Word by the Spirit, revelations in doctrine, in prophecy, in poems by the Holy Ghost in tongues with interpretation that He has given me, yet, above all the external evidences, that which God accomplishes in your own lives, demonstrating to your own consciousness the operations of God, no doubt is the great evidence to the believer himself, for that which is known in consciousness can not be denied. We stand firmly on scriptural grounds that every individual who is baptized in the Holy Ghost will and does speak in tongues.

Baptism means a degree of the Spirit upon the life sufficient to give the Spirit of God such absolute control of the person that He will be able to speak through him in tongues. Any lesser degree can not be called the Baptism or submersion, and we feel could properly be spoken of as an anointing. The life may be covered with deep anointings of the Holy Ghost yet not in sufficient degree to be properly called the Baptism.

6

THE BAPTISM OF THE HOLY GHOST: PART 4

The Baptism of the Holy Ghost is the greatest event in Christian history, greater than the crucifixion, of greater import than the resurrection, greater than the ascension, greater than the glorification. It was the end and finality of crucifixion and resurrection, ascension and glorification.

If Jesus Christ had been crucified and there had been no resurrection, His death would have been without avail, insofar as the salvation of mankind is concerned. Or if He had risen from the grave in resurrection, and failed to reach the throne of God, and receive from the Father the Gift of the Holy Ghost, the purpose for which He died, and for which He arose, would have been missed.

It is because there was no failure, it is because Jesus went to the ultimate, to the very Throne and heart of God, and secured right out of the heavenly treasury of the Eternal Soul, the Almighty Spirit, and poured it forth upon the world in divine baptism that we are here tonight.

The Day of Pentecost was the birthday of Christianity. Christianity never existed until the Holy Ghost came from heaven. The ministry of Jesus in the world was His own divine preparation of the world for His ultimate and final ministry. His ultimate and final ministry was to be BY THE SPIRIT.

The ministry of Jesus during His earth life was localized by His humanity, localized again in that His message was only given to Israel. But the descent of the Holy Ghost brought to the souls of men a UNIVERSAL ministry of Jesus to every man right from the heart of God. Heavenly contact with the eternal God in power set their nature all aflame for God and with God, exalted their natures into God, and made the recipient GODLIKE. Man became God-like!

There is no subject in all the Word of God that seems to me should be approached with so much holy reverence as the subject of the Baptism of the Holy Ghost. Beloved, my heart bleeds every day of my life when I hear the flippancy with which Christians discuss the Baptism of the Holy Ghost.

When Moses entered into the presence of God at the Burning Bush, God said, "Put off thy shoes from off thy feet, for the place whereon thou standest is holy ground." How much more so when the individual comes into the presence of God looking for the Baptism of the Holy Ghost, and remembers that in order to obtain this Gift, Jesus Christ lived in the world, bled on the cross, entered into the darkness of death and hell and the grave, grappled with and strangled that accursed power, came forth again, and finally ascended to heaven in order to secure it for you and me. If there is anything under heaven that ought to command our reverence, our Holy reverence, our reverence beyond anything else in the world, it surely is the subject of the Baptism of the Holy Ghost.

My! Sometimes my soul is jarred when I hear people flippantly say, "Have you got your baptism?" Supposing that Jesus was on the cross, and we were privileged tonight to look into His face at this hour, I wonder what the feeling of our soul would be? Supposing we were to follow tonight behind the weeping company that bore His dead body and laid it in the tomb, what would our feelings be? Supposing we were to meet Him in the garden, as Mary did, in the glory of His resurrection, or supposing that God in His goodness would let us look into that scene of scenes at the Throne of God, when the heavens lifted up their gates, and the Lord of Glory came in. Oh, if we could, beloved, we would have a better comprehension of the Baptism of the Holy Ghost.

I love that dear old word "Ghost." The Anglo-Saxon is "Ghest" a spiritual guest, heavenly visitor, spiritual presence, the Angel One. And that Angel One that comes to you and me, comes right out of the heart of the Eternal God, breathed through the soul of Jesus Christ! When He came upon a man originally, as He did upon the hundred and twenty at Jerusalem, no one went around saying: "Brother, have you got your baptism?" They were walking with their shoes off, with uncovered heads and uncovered hearts before the Eternal God!

I believe that the first essential in a real Holy Ghost Church and a real Holy Ghost work, is to begin to surround the Baptism of the Holy Ghost with that due reverence of God with which an experience so sacred, and that cost such an awful price, should be surrounded.

I sat one day on a kopje in South Africa, in company with a lady, Mrs. Dockrell, a beautiful woman of God, baptized in the Holy Ghost. As we sat together on the rocks, meditating and praying, the rest of the company being a little distance away, I observed the Spirit falling upon her powerfully, until she was submerged in the Spirit. Then she began to deliver a message, first in tongues, later giving the interpretation in English, and I listened to the most wonderful lecture on the subject of "REVERENCE" I have ever heard in all my life.

Afterward I said to her: "Tell me what you can about the experience through which you have just passed." She had never been in Europe. But she said, "I was carried by the Spirit somewhere in Europe. I approached a great cathedral." And she went on to describe its architecture. She said: "As I approached the door, I was greeted by an English priest, who led me down the isle to the altar, and I knelt. A white cloud began to settle down, and presently out of the cloud came the face and form of Jesus Christ. The priest was standing in the rostrum and began to speak but I could see by the action of the Spirit that the words he spoke were simply words that were being spoken by the Lord." It has always been one of the sorrows of my life that I did not have a stenographer, who could have taken that wonderful message on reverence for the works of God.

I have been reading one of the most beautiful books I have ever read. It is written by an English lady, Mrs. Parker, a missionary to India, and describes the life and teaching and mission of one Sadhu Sundar Singh, an Indian Sadhu. A Sadhu is a HOLY MAN, who renounces the world absolutely utterly, never marries, never takes part in any of the affairs of the world, separates himself to religious life, practices meditation on God and the spiritual life. Sundar Singh, when he found the Lord Jesus Christ, conceived the idea of becoming a Christian Sadhu. They walked from place to place. They wore no shoes, they slept on the ground, but their life is utterly abandoned to God.

One of the statements of Mrs. Parker, who wrote of Sundar Singh, was to this effect: "As you approach his presence, an awe comes over the soul. It seems as if you are again in the presence of the original Nazarene." Let us approach the Holy of Holies with a similar awe, Let us be reverential in the presence of the glorified One.

The Baptism of the Holy Ghost is peculiar to the Lord Jesus Christ. "I indeed," said John, "baptize you in water unto repentance, but HE shall baptize you with the Holy Ghost and with fire; whose fan is in

His hand, and He will thoroughly purge His floor, and gather His wheat into the garner; but He will burn up the chaff with unquenchable fire." Jesus Christ, the Glorified, must lay His hands on you and on me and bestow upon us all His own nature, the outflow of God, the substance of His soul, the quality of His mind, the very being of God Himself. "Know ye not that your body is the temple of the Holy Ghost, which is in you?" A temple of God, a house of God in which God lives!

Sometimes I have tried to get it clear before my soul that God LIVES IN ME. I have tried to note the incoming influence and power of that pure, sweet, living Spirit of the Eternal God. I have tried to realize His presence in my spirit, in my soul, in my hands, in my feet, in my person and being: a habitation of God, a habitation of God! God equipping the soul to minister, Himself, God, to the world. God equipping the soul of man that he may live forever in harmony of mind with God. God furnishing to the soul of man the POWER of His personality, by which man is as made as God. For all the God-like qualities of your heart is due to the fact that God by the Spirit dwells in you. What is it that you look for in another? It is God! You look into the eyes of another to see God. If you fail to see God in the other life, your heart is troubled. You were looking for God.

I am not interested in the form or the figure or the name of an individual. I am interested in seeing God. Is God there? Is God in that man? Is God in that woman? Is it God that speaks? Is it God that moves? Are You seeing God?

The Baptism of the Holy Ghost was the incoming of God in personality, in order that the man, through this force, might be moved by God. God lives in him, God speaks through him, God is the impulse of his soul, God has His dwelling place in him.

YOU may have God. That is the wonder of the Baptism of the Holy Ghost. It is not a work of grace, it is God possessing you. Oh, your heart may have been as sinful as the heart of man ever was sinful. But Christ comes to your soul. That spirit of darkness that possessed you goes, and in its stead, a new Spirit comes in, the Spirit of Christ. YOU have become a new creature, a saved man, a God-filled man.

Sin manifests itself in three ways, in thought, in acts, in nature. Salvation is a complete transformation. God takes possession of man, changes his thoughts, in consequence his acts change, his nature is new. A Christian is not a reformed man. A Christian is a man renewed, remade by the Spirit of God. A Christian is a man indwelt by God: the house of God, the tabernacle of the Most High! Man, indwelt by God, becomes the hands, and the heart, and the feet, and the mind of Jesus Christ. God descends into man, man ascends into God! That is the purpose and power of the Baptism in the Holy Ghost. A soul is saved. How does Jesus reach them? Through your hands, through your heart, through your faith. When God baptizes you in the Holy Ghost, He gives you the biggest gift that heaven or earth ever possessed. He gives you Himself! He joins you by the one Spirit to Himself forever.

The requirement is a surrendered heart, a surrendered mind, a surrendered life. From the day that a man becomes a child of God, baptized in the Holy Ghost, it was God's intention through Jesus Christ that that man should be a revelation or Jesus, not of himself any more. From that time on the Christian should be a revelation of Jesus.

If you were looking to know whether a man was baptized in the Holy Ghost or not, what would you look for? You would look for God in him. You would look for a revelation of the personality of God. God in him, God speaking in him, God speaking through him, God using his hands, God using his feet, a mind in harmony with God, a soul in touch with heaven, a spirit united and unified with and in Jesus Christ!

It is not in my heart to discourage any man, or to make you disbelieve for one minute in the trueness of your own baptism in the Holy Ghost. I believe that God by the Spirit has baptized many in the Holy Ghost. Hundreds and hundreds of people have been baptized in the Holy Ghost during the life of this Church in the last six years. But beloved, we have not comprehended the greatness of God's intent, Not that we have not received the Spirit, but our lives have not been sufficiently surrendered to God.

We must keep on ascending right to the Throne, right into the heart of God, right into the soul of the

Glorified.

The common teaching that my heart these days is endeavoring to combat is that God comes to present the individual with a gift of power, and the individual is then supposed to go out and manifest some certain characteristic of power. No! God comes to present you with HIMSELF. "Ye shall receive power after that the Holy Ghost is come upon you."

Jesus went to heaven in order that the very treasury of the heart of the Eternal God might be unlocked for your benefit, and that out of the very soul of the Eternal God, the streams of His life and nature would possess you from the crown of your head to the sole of your feet, and that there would be just as much of the Eternal God in your toe nails and in your brain as each are capable of containing. In other words, from the very soles of your feet to the last hair on the top of your heard, every cell of your being, would be a residence of the Spirit of the living God. Man is made alive by God and with God by the Spirit. And in the truest sense man is the dwelling place of God, the house of God, the tabernacle of the Most High.

Listen! "The words that I speak, I speak not of myself, but the Father that DWELLETH in Me." "But the Father that dwelleth in Me." Where did the Eternal Father dwell in Jesus Christ? Why in every part of His being, within and without, in the spirit of Him, in the soul of Him, in the brain of Him, in the body of Him, in the blood of Him, in the bones of

Him! Every single, solitary cell of His structure was the dwelling place of God, of God, OF GOD.

When you look for God you do not look on the surface. You look within. When you discern a man to see whether God is in him, you look into the spirit of him, into the soul of him, into the depth of him, and there you see God.

How trifling are the controversies that surround the Baptism of the Holy Ghost? Men are debating such trifling issues. For instance, does a man speak in tongues, or does he not? Do not think for a moment that I am discounting the value of tongues. I am not. But beloved, I will tell you what my heart is straining for. Down there at Jerusalem they not only spoke in tongues, but they spoke the languages of the NATIONS. If it was possible for old Peter and old Paul, or for the Jewish nation, then it is possible to every last one, Not to speak in tongues alone, as we ordinarily understand that phase, but to speak because God dwells in you and speaks to whomsoever and will in whatever language He desires. And if our present experience in tongues is not satisfying, God bless you, go on into languages, as God meant that you should. Dear ones, I feel the need of that, and I feel it away down in my heart to a depth that hurts. I lived in South Africa for a number of years, where it is commonly said that there are a hundred thousand tribes of native people. Every last one of the hundred thousand speaks a different dialect. These tribes number sometimes as low as ten thousand people and sometimes as high as hundreds of thousands, even millions, of people.

Supposing we were going to undertake to evangelize Africa rapidly. It would be necessary to have a hundred thousand different missionaries and have them all at one time, master one particular language, for there are a hundred thousand of them. No sir! I believe before High Heaven that when the Spirit of the Eternal God is poured out upon all flesh, that out of the real Christian body will arise a hundred thousand men and women in Africa that will speak in the language of every separate tribe by the power of God.

The unknown tongue of the Spirit was to teach you of God, to be a faith builder in your soul, to take you out into God's big practical endeavor to save the world. And that is the reason, dear ones, that I bring this issue to your soul tonight. In the matter of the Baptism of the Holy Ghost we are in a state of the merest infancy of understanding, the merest infancy of divine control, the merest infancy in ability to assimilate our environment, including languages.

When we go to a school we see classes arranged for every grade. I was talking to a young school teacher, who teaches out in the country in a little public school. I said: "How many children have you in your school?" She replied; "fifteen." I asked: "How many grades have you?" She said: "Eight grades." Fifteen scholars divided into eight grades.

The Christian Church is God's big school. What

student in the eighth grade would think of saying to the child learning its A, B, C's, "You haven't anything. Why don't you have the eighth grade understanding?" Well in due time he will have it. That is the reason the student does not say it. It is because he knows the child will have it. One day that boy will understand just the same as he does. A weak Christianity always wants to drop to the imperfect, and adjust itself to the popular mind. But a real Christianity ever seeks to be made perfect in God, both in character and gifts.

Dear ones, I want to repeat to you tonight a little of my own personal history on the subject of the Baptism of the Spirit, for I know it will clarify your soul.

I knelt under a tree when about sixteen years of age, in repentance and prayer, and God came into my soul. I was saved from my sins, and from that day I knew Jesus Christ as a living Savior. There never was a single moment of question about the reality of His incoming into my life as a Savior, for He saved me from my sins. My friends said, "You are baptized in the Holy Ghost."

Sometime later, I think when I was yet under twenty, or there-about, I met a Christian farmer, Nelvin Pratt, who sat down on his plough handles and taught me the subject of sanctification, and God let me enter into that experience. My friends said: "Now surely you are baptized in the Holy Ghost." Later in my life I came under the ministry of George B. Watson, of the Christian and Missionary Alliance, who taught with more clearness and better distinction between the Baptism of the Holy Ghost and sanctification, and I entered into a richer life and a better experience. A beautiful anointing of the Spirit was upon my life.

When the ministry of Healing was opened to me, and I ministered for ten years. in the power of God. Hundreds and hundreds of people were healed by the power of God during this ten years, and I could feel the conscious flow of the Holy Spirit through my soul and my hands.

But at the end of that ten years I believe I was the hungriest man for God that ever lived. There was such a hunger for God that as I left my offices in Chicago and walked down the street, my soul would break out, and I would cry, "Oh God!" I have had people stop and look at me in wonder. It was the yearning passion of my soul, asking for God in a greater measure than I then knew. But my friends would say: "Mr. Lake, you have a beautiful baptism in the Holy Ghost." Yes, it was nice as far as it went, but it was not answering the cry of my heart. I was growing up into a larger understanding of God and my own souls need. My soul was demanding a greater entrance into God, His love, presence and power.

And then one day an old man strolled into my office, sat down, and in the next half hour he revealed more of the knowledge of God to my soul than I had ever known before. And when he passed out I said: "God bless that old grey head. That man knows more of God than any man I ever met. By the grace of God, if that is what the Baptism of the Holy Ghost with tongues does, I am going to possess it." Oh, the wonder of God that was then revealed to my heart!

I went into fasting and prayer and waiting on God for nine months. And one day the glory of God in a new manifestation and a new incoming came to my life. And when the phenomena had passed, and the glory of it remained in my soul, I found that my life began to manifest in the varied range of the gifts of the Spirit. And I spoke in tongues by the power of God, and God flowed through me with a new force. Healings were of a more powerful order. Oh, God lived in me, God manifested in me, God spoke through me. My spirit was deified, and I had a new comprehension of God's will, new discernment of spirit, new revelation of God in me. For nine months everything that I looked at framed itself into poetic verse. I could not look at the trees without it framing itself into a glory poem of praise. I preached to audiences of thousands night after night and day after day. People came from all over the world to study me. They could not understand. Everything I said was a stream of poetry. It rolled from my soul in that form. My spirit had become a fountain of poetic truth.

Then a new wonder was manifested. My nature became so sensitized that I could lay my hands on any man or woman and tell what organ was diseased, and to what extent, and all about it. I tested it. I went to hospitals where physicians could not diagnose a case, touched a patient and instantly I knew the organ that was diseased, its extent and condition and location. And one day it passed away. A child gets to playing with a toy, and his joy is so wonderful he sometimes forgets to eat.

Oh say, don't you remember when you were first baptized in the Holy Ghost, and you first spoke in tongues, how you bubbled and babbled, it was so wonderful, so amazing? We just wanted to be babies and go on bubbling and exhilarating. And now we are wondering what is the matter. The effervescence seems to have passed away. My! It is a good thing that it did. God is letting your soul down, beloved, into the bedrock. Right down where your mind is not occupied any more with the manifestation of God. God is trying to get your mind occupied with HIMSELF. God has come into you, now He is drawing you into Himself.

Will you speak in tongues when you are baptized in the Holy Ghost? Yes, you will, but you will do an awful lot more than that, bless God. An awful lot more than that! You will speak with the soul of Jesus Christ. You will feel with the heart of the Son of God. Your heart will beat with a heavenly desire to bless the world, because it is the pulse of Jesus that is throbbing in your soul. And I do not believe there will be a bit of inclination in your heart to turn around another child of God and say: "You are not in my class. I am baptized with the Holy Ghost." That is as foreign to the Spirit of the Son of God as night is from day. Beloved, if you are baptized in the Holy Ghost, there will be a tenderness in your soul so deep that you will never crush the aspiration of another by a single suggestion, but your soul will throb and beat and pulse in love, and your heart will be under that one to lift it up to God and push it out as far into the glory as your faith can send it.

I want to talk with the utmost frankness, and say to you, that tongues have been to me the making of my ministry. It is that peculiar communication with God when God reveals to my soul the truth I utter to you day by day in my ministry. But that time of communication with me is mostly in the night. Many a time I climb out of bed, take my pencil and pad and jot down the beautiful things of God, the wonderful things of God, that He talks out in my spirit and reveals to my heart.

Many Christians do not understand the significance of tongues, any more than the other man understands the experience of your soul when you are saved from sin. It has taken place in you. It is in your heart, it is in your mind, it is in your being. The man who tries to make you doubt the reality of your touch with God when He saved you out of your sin is foolish. It is established IN you. The old Methodists could not explain the experience, but they said: "It is better felt that told." They knew it by internal knowledge. So it is in a real baptism of the Holy Ghost. So it is in prophecy. So it is in healing. So it is in tongues. Do not throw away what you have. Go on to perfection.

THE SPIRIT OF MAN HAS A VOICE. Do you get that? The spirit of man has a voice. The action of God in your spirit causes your spirit to speak by its voice. In order to make it intelligent to your understanding it has to be repeated in the language that your brain knows. Why? Because there is a language common to the spirit of man, and it is not English, and it is not German, and it is not French, and it is not Italian, or any other of the languages of earth. It is a language of the spirit of man. And, oh, what a joy it was when that pent-up, bursting, struggling spirit of yours found it's voice and "spake in tongues."

Many a time I have talked to others in the Spirit, by the Spirit, through the medium of tongues, and knew everything that was said to me, but I did not know it with this ear. It was not the sound of their words. It was that undefinable something that made it intelligent. Spirit speaks to spirit, just as mouth speaks to mouth, or as man speaks to man. Your spirit speaks to God. God is Spirit. He answers back. Bless God. And I believe with all my heart that is what Paul had in mind when he talked about the "unknown" tongue. The unknown tongue, that medium of internal revelation of God to you. The common language of the spirit of man, by which God communicates with your spirit.

But if you want to make that medium of internal revelation of God intelligent to other folks, then it must be translated into the language that they know. That is the reason the apostle says: "Let him that speaketh in tongues pray that he may interpret," that the Church may receive edifying. Paul says: "IN THE CHURCH I would rather speak five words with my understanding, that by my voice I might teach others also, than ten thousand words in an unknown tongue." Your revelation from God is given to you in tongues, but you give it forth in the language the people understand.

Beloved, settle it. It is one of the divine mediums and methods of communication between your spirit and God's. And as long as you live, when you talk about TONGUES, speak with reverence, for it is God. When you talk about healing, speak with reverence, for it is God. When you talk about prophecy, remember it is God.

A German woman came to the healing rooms one day and a brother prayed for her. She had been a school teacher, but had to give up her profession because of her eye sight. She came back some weeks late after having been alone for three weeks. She had never been in a religious service in her life where they speak in tongues, and had not knowledge of the Scriptures on that line. She came back to me with a volume of written material that God had given her. For when she had been prayed for to receive healing, the Spirit of God came upon her and she was baptized in the Holy Ghost. And now God had commenced to reveal Himself to her, teach her of

His Word, and of His will, until she filled a volume with written material of her conversations with God. She communed with God in tongues, her spirit speaking to God, but when she came to me I received it in English.

The man that sits along side of you can not understand that. He never talked to God. He does not understand anything about getting up in the middle of the night to write down what God has said to him. Well, he needs something else to convince him that there is a God. Tongues are for a sign, NOT to them that believe, but to them that believe not. But prophecy, the outspeaking for God, is for all. Therefore, Paul does not want them to crush a man who is speaking in tongues, but to keep their hands off and stand back. Leave him alone with God. Let him travel away out in His love and power, and come back with messages in his soul.

But he must not monopolize the time of hundreds of people in the Church with a private communication of God to his soul. But when he has completed his interview with God, he gives forth his knowledge as interpretation or prophecy.

There have been so many controversies over the various gifts of the Spirit as they appeared one after another. Twenty-five or thirty years ago when we began in the ministry of Healing, we had to fight to keep from being submerged by our opposing brethren in Jesus Christ, who thought you were insane because you suggested that the Lord Jesus Christ could still heal. In the State of Michigan I had to go into the courts to keep some of my friends out of the insane asylum because they believed God could heal without taking pills or some other material stuff.

It was because they did not understand the eternal and invisible nature of God. They had no idea God could be ministered through a man's hands and soul, fill a sick man's body, take possession of and make him whole. The world has had to learn this. It is a science far in advance of so-called material or physical science.

Then that marvelous wave of God came over the country from 1900 to 1906, when hundreds of thousands of people were baptized in the Holy Ghost and spoke in tongues. But listen! Old John Alexander Dowie, riding on the wave of that wonderful manifestation of healing power, wanted to build a Church and stamp it with healing only, and his Church practically did that, and died. Other Churches branded theirs with Holiness only, and died. Others with an anointing of the Holy Ghost, called "baptism," and they died in power also. Later on we wanted to build a great structure and stamp it with tongues. After a while the tongues got dry. Somehow the glory and the glow had gone out of them. They became rattly and did not sound right. What was the matter? Nothing wrong with the experience. God had not departed from the life, but was hidden from our view. We were absorbed in phenomena of God, and not in God Himself. Now we must go on. Now beloved, I can see as my spirit discerns the future and reaches out to touch the heart of mankind, and the desire of God, that there is coming from heaven a new manifestation of the Holy Ghost in power, and that new manifestation will be in sweetness, in love, in tenderness, in the power of the Spirit, beyond anything your heart or mine ever saw. The very lightning of God will flash through men's soul. The sons of God will meet the sons of darkness and prevail. Jesus Christ will destroy anti-Christ.

In 1908, I preached at Pretoria, South Africa, when one night God came over my life in such power, in such streams of liquid glory and powers that it flowed consciously off my hands like streams of electricity, I would point my finger at a man, and that stream would strike him. When a man interrupted the meeting, I would point my finger at him and say: "Sit down!" He fell as if struck, and lay for three hours. When he became normal they asked him what happened, and he said, "Something struck me that went straight through me, I thought I was shot."

At two o'clock in the morning I ministered to sixty-five sick who were present. And the streams of God that were pouring through my hands were so powerful the people would fall as though they were hit. I was troubled because they fell with such violence. And the Spirit said: "You do not need to put your hands on them. Keep your hands a distance away." And when I held my hands a foot from their heads they would crumple and fall in a heap on the floor. They were healed, almost every one.

That was the outward manifestation. That was what the people saw. But beloved, something transpired in my heart that made my soul like the soul of Jesus Christ. Oh, there was such a tenderness, a new-born tenderness of God, that was so wonderful that my heart reached out and cried and wept over men in sin. I could gather them in my arms and love them, and Jesus Christ flowed out of me and delivered them. Drunkards were saved and healed as they stood transfixed looking at me.

During that period men would walk down the aisle, and when they came within ten feet of me, I have seen them fall prostrate, one on top of the other. A preacher who had sinned, as he looked at me fell prostrate, was saved, baptized in the Holy Ghost, and stirred the nation with his message of love.

In eighteen months God raised up one hundred white Churches in the land. That hundred Churches was born in my tabernacle at Johannesburg. The multitude of those who composed that hundred Churches were healed or baptized in the Holy Ghost under my own eyes, as I preached or prayed.

I continued in the ministry of healing until I saw hundreds of thousands healed. At last I became tired. I went on healing people day after day, as though I were a machine. And all the time my heart kept asking: "Oh God, let me know yourself better. I want you, my heart wants YOU, God." Seeing men saved and healed and baptized in the Holy Most did not satisfy my growing soul. It was crying for a greater consciousness of God, the within-ness of me was yearning for Christ's own life and love. After a while my soul reached the place where I said: "If I can not get God into my soul to satisfy the soul of me, all the rest of this is empty." I had lost interest in it, but if I put my hands on the sick they continued to be healed by the power of God.

I will never forget Spokane, Washington, for during the first six months I was there, God satisfied the cry of my heart, and God came in and my mind opened and my spirit understood afresh, and I was able to tell of God and talk out the heart of me like I never had been able to before. God reached a new depth in my spirit, and revealed new possibilities in God. So beloved, you pray through. Pray through for this Church, pray through for this work. Oh! God will come! God will come with more tongues than you have ever heard. God will come with more power than your eyes ever beheld. God will come with waves of heavenly love and sweetness, and blessed be God, your heart will be satisfied in Him.

Will a man speak in tongues when he is baptized in the Holy Ghost? Yes, he will, and he will heal the sick when he is baptized, and he will glorify God out of the spirit of him, with praises more delightful and heavenly than you ever heard. And he will have a majestic bearing. He will look like the Lord Jesus Christ, and he will be like Him. Blessed be God.

The greatest manifestation of the Holy Ghost

baptized life ever given to the world was not in the preaching of the apostles, it was not in the wonderful manifestations of God that took place at their hands. It was in the UNSELFISHNESS manifested by the Church. Think of it! Three thousand Holy Ghost baptized Christians in Jerusalem from the Day of Pentecost onward, who loved their neighbors' children as much as their own, who were so anxious for fear their brethren did not have enough to eat, that they sold their estates, and brought the money and laid it at the apostles feet, and said: "Distribute it. Carry the glow and the fire and the wonder of this divine salvation to the whole world." That showed what God had wrought in their hearts. Oh, I wish we could arrive at that place, where this Church was baptized in that degree of unselfishness.

That would be a greater manifestation than Healing, greater than conversion, greater than baptism in the Holy Ghost, greater than tongues. It would be a manifestation of the LOVE of 1 Corinthians 13, that so many preach about, and do not possess. When a man sells his all for God, and distributes it for the Kingdom's good, it will speak louder of love than the evangelists who harp about love, and oppose tongues and the other gifts of the Spirit.

That was the same Holy Ghost that came upon them and caused them to speak in tongues. No more grabbing for themselves. No more bantering for the biggest possible salary, no more juggling to put themselves and their friends in the most influential positions. All the old characteristics were gone. They were truly saved. Why, their heart was like the heart of Jesus, their soul was like the soul of God, they loved as God loved, they loved the world, they loved sinners so that they gave their all to save them.

Do you want Him? You can have Him. Oh! He will come and fill your soul. Oh, the Holy Ghost will take possession of your life. He will reveal the wonder of heaven and the glory of God, and the richness and purity of His holiness, and make you sweet and God-like forever.

Prayer in Tongues and Interpretation

Thou art not far away, Oh God. Our souls tonight are enveloped in the Eternal God. We feel thee round about us. We feel thy precious loving arm, and the beating of thy heart, and the pulsing of thy heavenly soul, and we are asking thee, my God, that the truth of the Eternal shall be breathed into us forever until all our nature is submerged in God, buried up in God, infilled with God, revealing God.

7

BUILDING ON A FIRM FOUNDATION

"Ye shall receive power, after that the Holy Ghost is come upon you." We are entitled to it, bless God. We are glad to see some of it and wish, bless God, that we might see a great deal more. And beloved, I have a splendid conviction in my heart that we will.

I want to read some familiar verses, as a basis of thought.

"When Jesus came into the coasts of Caesarea Philippi, he asked his disciples, saying, 'Whom do men say that I the Son of man am?'

"And they said, 'Some say that thou art John the Baptist: some, Elias; and others, Jeremias, or one of the prophets.'

"He saith unto them, 'But whom say ye that I am?'

"And Simon Peter answered and said, 'Thou art the Christ, the Son of the living God.'

"And Jesus answered and said unto him, 'Blessed art thou, Simon Barjona: for flesh and blood hath not revealed it unto thee, but my Father which is in heaven. And I say also unto thee, That thou art Peter, and upon this rock I will build my church; and the gates of hell shall not prevail against it.'" (Matthew 16:13-18)

Those of us who are familiar with this scripture will remember that Peter is very careful to call attention to the fact that Jesus wasn't referring to him as the one upon which the Church was to be built. He speaks in the second chapter of First Peter of how Jesus Christ is the great foundation and is established upon the apostles and prophets, Jesus Christ Himself being the chief cornerstone, etc.

Foundation laying is always a hard process. Over here in the East, with your solid ground, you are not so badly as some cities in the West, Chicago, for example. Chicago is built on a great quicksand bed, which is from seventy to eighty feet deep. After the great Chicago fire, the board of aldermen did a thing that no body of men had ever dared to do till then. They passed an ordinance raising the grade of the city sixteen feet. In sections of the city where the old buildings still stand, you go down a story and a half from the street level to the original street. It was a tremendous undertaking, but it got them everlastingly out of the mud. So sometimes a destructive process is good. The Chicago fire became the great means by which the new and wonderful city came into existence.

I want to talk to you today about foundation building. When I was a young man I was a builder. I looked upon Chicago as the great Mecca of all builders, so I got to Chicago as quick as I could. I looked around among various occupations and I settled on this fact: There were two classes of men always in demand: the man who understood scientific foundation building, and the man who understood scientific roofing. And I said, "I will master these two things."

In those days, they used to build twelve story skyscrapers, sometimes fourteen. Foundation building was not known as it is today. In those days they went to the forests and brought great pilings, seventy, eighty, and ninety feet long. These were driven into the ground until they touched bedrock. At the surface, these were cut off level and railroad iron laid on top. Then they commenced their stone work on top of the railroad iron, and after they got to the street level it would probably be brick.

I lived long enough to see that these great buildings would get out of plumb and it would be necessary for a civil engineer to go over the buildings every three months to see whether they were moving out of plumb one way or another. If they were, great systems of jackscrews were used under the buildings to adjust them. It may surprise some of you to know that some of these great buildings in Chicago would literally stand on a system of jackscrews, which are adjusted every three months by civil engineers. That was too much like hanging a city up in the air, so they said, "We will drive great steel castings down to the rock and we will take out the earth and fill the castings with cement." That system likewise passed away. And now they excavate clear down to the bedrock, four or five stories if necessary. The quicksand and mud is removed. The foundation is laid on the base rock.

For the Church of God and Christian faith to become strong and to be built up in God, it is necessary to get a good foundation. It is a greater problem with most builders to get the old rubbish out of the way than to do the building. If we will look at our own lives, we will observe this: that the things that have been rooted and grounded in our hearts—some tradition of the Fathers, some of it misconception of the meaning of the Word of God; much of our teaching is fragmented—these form the greatest obstacles to the engrafting of the living Word of God. Every one of us who have progressed in God have found that the difficulty was not in believing the Word of God, but the difficulty was to get away from things that were settled in our own being as facts, though untrue. How hardly have we struggled over the matter of, "If it be Thy will," concerning sickness. From our babyhood and all down through the generations, we have been taught that if you are sick, the proper thing to do is to pray, "If it be Thy will," forgetting all the time that the Lord has forever demonstrated and declared His eternal will concerning the subject of sickness by healing all that come to Him.

Well, bless God, some have succeeded in getting over that difficulty and put the subject, "If it be Thy will," behind their back and moved out where they believe the declarations of Jesus Christ. So it was that victory came on that line.

Now dear ones, the thing that the Spirit of God is laying deeply upon my own heart these days is the need of a settled, established state in the Lord Jesus Christ, and the movement of the Spirit worldwide is to bring into unity the children of God who will raise A Standard of Truth for the World.

Now listen! This come-together call of the Spirit is not an isolated movement. It doesn't belong to a little company of people in Philadelphia, nor in any other city. In the last days, months, or the last year, in my correspondence worldwide, I have discovered this quote and the Lord is beginning to move everywhere in this particular line. Only yesterday I received a letter from Los Angeles from one of the prominent leaders. He goes on to outline the processes of development in God through which he has been brought during the last few years and its final result. I had written of what God was doing in our own midst and what God was endeavoring to do in the establishment of the Church, etc. He said, "Brother, your letter is a revelation. We thought that was all confined to ourselves, but I see that this movement, that we supposed was local, is a general movement, and of the Holy Ghost, and it is in your heart just as it has been in ours."

So God is moving in these days on a certain definite line. The man who has a settled, established faith in God has got that faith based on the eternal declarations of the Lord Jesus Christ and is moving in harmony with the revealed plan of God as outlined for this hour in God's Church Plan. The difficulty with most individuals and teachers in times past has been that the revelation of the mind of God, as revealed in the Word, was limited to such a degree that they were compelled to take only a certain few of the great principles of the Gospel, and thus their entire system was based on them. But in these days, as the coming of the Lord approaches and as the added light of the Spirit has been given, God has revealed in a larger way, in a broader manner, the truth. So that in these days it seems to me it is the purpose of God that the Church of the latter day, the Church of Philadelphia (if you like), should be based upon the great broad basis of the eternal truth, as laid down in the New Testament by the Lord Jesus Christ and the apostles, not on any fragmentary principles.

In days past, it was thought necessary to endeavor to bind men's hearts and consciences to certain established truths that the Church was ready to accept. And so these truths were usually embodied in the form of a creed, and they said, "This is all of truth that we accept. This is our faith." So they laid this basis and built a fence around themselves. After awhile, to the amazement of the Church and to her discomfiture, it was discovered that their creeds have been the means that squeezed them in, and instead of being a foundation broad enough for the Word of God, they are strangled inside their unyielding creed and there is no room for expansion. When the dear Lord has wanted to give a revelation of progressive truth, He has been compelled to go outside of the Church fence and raise up a new body. That was because a fence had been built. A certain little enunciation of truth had been collected and the structure established on that instead of on the entire Word of God.

We can see this: The individual who learns truth these days cannot confine it to certain declarations of doctrines. For as the days go by we see the progressive light of God, and if you were to compare your faith now with what you believed ten years ago, you would find there has been a great expansion. Now what is ten years more going to develop? What truths will it be necessary for us ourselves to accept from the Lord in the coming days? Consequently, beloved, there is only one basis upon which the Church of Jesus Christ can rest: That is, upon Jesus Christ and the apostles and the whole body of truth as outlined in the New Testament.

Then, beloved, in that great body of truth there must be the accompanying largeness and Spirit of the Lord Jesus Christ who didn't confine Himself to certain little dogmatic teachings, but He laid the great broad principles upon which the whole great kingdom of heaven rests and upon which a great Christian life can rest eternally.

There never was a teacher like Jesus. He was the one great Mastermind who understood the Spirit of the living God, who understood that all revelation of God was a progressive revelation. And thereby the minds that He must prepare by His own personal teaching were not able to receive all the great body of truth He had to reveal, so He said, "Ye are not able to bear it now." They had to grow up into the place in God where they were able to bear and analyze and utilize the greater truths of the Word of God. Now, beloved, we are in the place, just that place, bless God.

I believe in my heart that God is laying, even in this little company with her one hundred and twenty like the church at Jerusalem, the foundation of the truth of God that will command the attention of the Christian world.

Yesterday I received an invitation from E. N. Bell, Editor of Word & Witness, Malvern, Arkansas. In April they are having a great convention down there that includes all the Southern states. Among other things he says, "Brother Lake, there are two contending forces; the one which desires a strong organization, the other which don't want any organization, but desires to be a law unto themselves."

As I read the letter I said, "They are both wrong." The man who is an anarchist and is a law unto himself and doesn't put himself into line with the Word and cooperate with God according to God's plan is just as great a sinner as the other who comes along and wants to organize the Church into a frozen, man-created mass.

Jesus Christ laid down the principles of eternal truth: Every man who accepts the principles, who lives the life, is acceptable to Me. So, beloved, the Church of God these latter days must just return to the blessed basis that the Lord Jesus Christ laid down.

Beloved, the day has long gone past when men's consciences can be bound with certain little doctrines. If we were to take this audience today, of those who are living holy lives, baptized in the Holy Ghost, and note carefully what this brother believes and that brother believes, we would perhaps have twenty different statements before you got through with this little company.

Don't you see, the thing is this: Our hearts are one in the blood of Jesus Christ, our hearts are one in the recognition of a common Spirit of God. Blessed be His name! Every one of us can join hands and hearts on the seven unities demanded and experienced in the Church at Ephesus, "One body, one Spirit, one hope, one Lord, one faith, one baptism, one God and Father of you all, who is above all, through all, and in you all." (Ephesians 4:4-6)

So the dear Lord, in these days, is once again moving upon the hearts of men that the body of Jesus Christ shall be brought together in holy oneness, that the power of God may be poured upon her, that the Spirit of the living God may move through her in mighty power and demonstration, and that through her the last message of this present age may be given to the world, the great kingdom message. Bless God.

It seems to me we are only beginning to understand with what force the kingdom message is going to come and its revolutionary character. A few weeks ago the country was stirred by one man's endeavor to just touch in a small way the first principle of Jesus Christ, that first one, "Blessed are the poor in spirit." I refer to Henry Ford, the manufacturer of the Ford Motor car. He set aside out of his profit, ten million dollars for 1914, to be divided between his twenty-six thousand employees. He established a minimum wage of five dollars per day to be the wage of every man. Then every two weeks, he would receive in a check the proportionate amount of the ten million dollars, in addition to his wages.

We say, "Bless God, that is a good thing." That's a starting point. It indicates that some men are beginning to see the mind of the Lord. It is not by any means a fulfillment [illegible]. Then the selfish man says, "Yes, that will draw to Henry Ford every expert workman in the United States, etc. and his profits thereby will only be increased, not lessened, but it is a start."

Now see, the blessed principles of the Lord Jesus Christ are the principles of unselfishness. That is the one crowning principle that the Lord Jesus Christ wants to lay down in His Church this very day. It makes no difference how it is applied. The Lord Jesus Christ Himself didn't undertake to tell us how to apply that principle. He left it to every man in his own station. But, beloved, the demand upon us is that we live that blessed principle of the Lord Jesus Christ.

My thought is this: Jesus Himself didn't undertake to tell us dogmatically how to apply that principle, but He, on the other hand, laid down the principles and left it to us, His sovereign servants, to apply them just as the Spirit of the Lord illuminated our own hearts and told us to do. That is the great basis upon which the Lord Jesus Christ is founding His Church. It is based on the principles of the Son of God. He doesn't ask us what we think about this or that petty doctrine, but He lays down the great principles of the kingdom as the essentials:

1. "Blessed are the poor in spirit: for theirs is the kingdom of heaven."

2. "Blessed are they that mourn: for they shall be comforted."

3. "Blessed are the meek: for they shall inherit the earth."

4. "Blessed are they which do hunger and thirst after righteousness: for they shall be filled."

5. "Blessed are the merciful: for they shall obtain mercy."

6. "Blessed are the pure in heart: for they shall see God."

7. "Blessed are the peacemakers: for they shall be called the children of God."

8. "Blessed are they which are persecuted for

righteousness' sake: for theirs is the kingdom of heaven."

Beloved, these are the things that God calls us back to today: to the original basis, to the foundation: Jesus Christ Himself, the chief cornerstone. We see these blessed principles exemplified all through the New Testament by the apostles themselves, who as the fathers of the Church, were desirous that they should not even become a burden on the Church and endeavored to keep themselves from being a burden. And with their own hands in some instances labored that they might have the privilege of living and preaching the blessed Gospel of the Lord Jesus Christ.

Don't you see, beloved, that every departure from the principles that the Lord Jesus has laid down has weakened the great fabric? Out of that condition has grown our divisions. All our departure from the principles of the Lord has robbed us of that vital faith that was necessary to get answers from God, even for our daily bread. A return to the principles of the Lord Jesus Christ, to the practical life of the Son of God, will bring again upon our souls the blessing of God.

Beloved, that's the entrance into power. That's the final manner of testing the spirit. The spirit must ever be tested by the Word of God, by the principles of Jesus Christ; the law that He laid down by the commandments of Jesus. If the spirit in you won't measure up with the principles that the Lord Jesus Christ laid down, be sure that it is not the Spirit of the Lord Jesus Christ. If the spirit in you exalts itself, etc., just settle it. There is a spirit there that isn't like the Spirit of the Lord Jesus. The way we can see what His Spirit was like is from the principles He laid down and the life He lived.

I feel it this day that the Lord is going to pour a rich and wonderful blessing upon the saints when we come down and return to the blessed principles of the Gospel of Jesus.

If I were to advise you to do anything particular during the coming weeks it would be this: Take the fifth, sixth, and seventh of Matthew and read them and reread them on your knees, until the principles of Jesus Christ enter into your heart. Then, bless God, there will be a good basis laid in your soul for the everlasting blessing of God.

It is as impossible to get the eternal working power of God to appear in a man's life, or the life of the Church, until first the clearing away is done and the rubbish of petty doctrine and littleness is taken out of the way, as it would be to build a Chicago skyscraper without first taking out all the quicksand and mass of rotten stuff. It has got to come out. It has got to be cleared away. When the life goes down on the eternal Rock, Jesus Christ, then the structure will come up and will stand in the power of God.

So this morning I pray God that He will help us this day to take these blessed words of God, the declarations of Jesus Himself as He has outlined them in the fifth, sixth, and seventh of Matthew especially, and get these real basic things settled in our soul.

I have received during the week applications from several persons who want to come up here and receive membership into this body, who desire to receive the right hand of fellowship. You can't keep it from growing, from developing. But O, beloved, is it going to develop in God or is it going to be like every institution has been or is it going to be placed on eternal foundations? And is our life going down into the bottom, to the bedrock, to the foundation stone of Christ Jesus?

Let us pray.

O God, our Father, let our lives be once and forever and for all settled on the eternal Rock, Christ Jesus, Lord God, where our lives shall stand. Blessed be Thy name! And where the Church of Jesus Christ shall stand, Lord God, and the gates of hell shall not prevail against her. Blessed be Thy name! O God, let that deep, true, holy, unselfish working of the Holy Ghost in our lives be so pure and true and real that, my God, there shall not be left a superficial thing in us, Lord, but that our character shall be opened wide, opened to the living God, and wide open to one another. O God, reflecting, showing forth the real life of Jesus Christ. O God, we bless Thee for this day. Lord God, there is an echo of gladness in our soul. There is a shout of praise in our hearts. Lord God, the day has come. Thine appointed hour has come when Thou hast really begun to call together into one body the body members of Jesus Christ whose names are written in heaven. Lord God, we worship at Thy feet, and Lord, we declare our faith in Thee, the Son of God, this very day. Thou art going to bring forth Thy people, Lord God, the Church of Jesus Christ, bless God! Who shall give forth to the world the message of the kingdom. Bless God! Who shall raise up a banner of truth and demonstrate a righteousness that men of God will not have to be ashamed of.

O God, we pray Thee then, that the great virtue of Jesus Christ shall be so inwrought in us that, my God and Father, we shall look with love into the face of every other man. That, O God, our Father, we will have the eyes of Jesus in us and the heart of Jesus in us in such a way that we will not see things that are evil, but O God, we will see the good in the man. We will see the purity, Lord, we will think of the things that are lovely, Lord, and are true, Lord. We will be so pure and clean before God that the light of God and the life of God shall shine in us and flow through us so that mankind will be blessed.

O God, our Father, we rejoice in this day. We rejoice in this hour. Thou art the Son of God, Lord Jesus. We are so glad You have let us live at this time of life. My God, we rejoice in the expectation of Thy soon coming. Bless God! But O Jesus, blessed Jesus, get us ready, get us ready. Lord God, get us ready to give the message that is going to stir the world. Get us ready, Lord, to receive the power of God that is going to demonstrate Christ to mankind, for Jesus' sake.

O God, we pray that upon this Pentecostal Movement worldwide and upon the Church of Christ at large, by whatever name it is known and upon the hidden ones who are known by no name, the power of God shall come. Lord God, once again let the pulsating movement of the Holy Ghost be felt through the body of Christ. Lord Jesus, draw Thy children together, Lord. Lord Jesus, establish them on the rock. Lord God, build up the body, we pray Thee, Lord. And bless God, we pray that upon our own souls these days there shall be such a passion of the Christ-heart that we will seek the lost, that we will seek the sick, that, my God, religious life, religious service shall forever cease to be a matter of religious entertainment. But O God, make it what Your heart desires, religious service, serving our fellowmen. O God, shedding Your tears with the afflicted, putting Your hands under the weary, lifting them up to God, praying for the stricken ones.

O Christ, let the pure heart and Spirit of Christ throb in every breast for Jesus' sake, that the will of God may come, that the prayer of Jesus Christ may be answered, that we may all be one. Lord God, that Thy kingdom may come and Thy will be done in earth as it is in heaven, Lord, for Jesus' sake. Amen.

8

MOSES' REBUKE

Moses had his interview with the Lord at the burning bush, and God had definitely commanded him to go to Pharaoh in Egypt and demand the deliverance of the children of Israel. God gave him the signet of His presence with him, his shepherd rod. All the miracles that followed that demand had taken place, and the children of Israel were finally given permission by the king to leave.

They started toward the Red Sea when the king's heart drew back, and I presume he felt he had done an unwise thing. He was losing the services of two and a half, probably four million slaves. In his effort to recall what he had done, he started after them with an army. In the meantime, Moses had gotten down to the Red Sea. On the right and on the left were impassable mountains and Pharaoh and his armies behind him.

The situation from a natural point of view was desperate, and if there was ever a time when a man was seemingly justified in calling on God in prayer, it was then. But I want to show you tonight one of the things I regard as a hindrance in our life for God. Most of us do just exactly what Moses did. When the test comes we stop and cry and as a second thing we stop and pray and put ourselves in a position where we become amenable to exactly the same rebuke that came upon Moses.

Moses started to pray. It is not recorded how long he prayed, or what he said, but instead of God being pleased, He was grieved and said to Moses: "Why standest thou here, and criest unto Me? Speak to the children of Israel that they go forward." I will turn to the Scripture and read the exact words:

"The Lord said unto Moses, 'Wherefore criest thou unto me? speak unto the children of Israel, that they go forward: But lift thou up thy rod, and stretch out thine hand over the sea, and divide it: and the children of Israel shall go on dry ground through the midst of the sea.'" (Exodus 14:15-16)

God did not even say, "You stretch out your hand, and I will divide the sea." But God said to Moses: "Stretch out thine hand over the sea, and divide it." It was not an act for God to perform, but it was an act for Moses to believe for. The responsibility was not with God: it was with Moses. A weak Christianity is ever inclined to whine in prayer while God waits for the believer to command it.

In my judgment, that is the place of extreme weakness in Christian character. I feel that very frequently prayer is made a refuge to dodge the action of faith. And just exactly as Moses came down there and began to pray instead of honoring God's word to him by the use of his rod, so many times our prayer becomes offensive to God. Because instead of praying as Moses did, God demands us to stretch forth our hand, exercise our rod of faith, and divide the waters.

In many respects it seems to me, this is the most powerful lesson that the Word of God contains on the subject of prayer and faith. Just stop for a moment and think of God throwing the responsibility of making a passage through the sea on Moses. God would not take it. It was for Moses to believe God and act. God commands: "Lift up thy rod, and stretch out thine hand," not "My hand." He was to lift the rod that God had given to him, the signet of God's presence with him to be used by the hand of Moses.

In the consideration of the whole subject of an Apostolic Church, do you not see the principle in it? The principle of acceptance of responsibility from God.

I want to call your attention now to the New Testament on that line. In the ninth chapter of Luke we have Jesus commanding the twelve disciples:

"Then he called his twelve disciples together, and gave them power and authority over all devils, and to cure diseases. And he sent them to preach the kingdom of God, and to heal the sick."

Moses stood before God, and God gave him the

commission to go down to Egypt. Then as an evidence of His presence, He said, "What is it you have in your hands?"

Moses answered, "A rod."

He said, "Throw it down," and as Moses obeyed it became a serpent.

Then He said, "Take it up," and it was changed to a rod again. This is one of the instances of taking up serpents. God said, "Keep it. It is a signet of My presence with you," and it was so with Moses.

But you see Moses had forgotten as he stood by the Red Sea, that God had given him a sign of His presence with him. Circumstances overpowered him and he commenced to pray and that prayer was an offense to God.

Just as God had done with Moses, so Jesus called the twelve to Him, and gave them power and authority over all devils, and to cure diseases, and that was their rod. He sent them to preach the kingdom of God and heal the sick. Suppose they came to the sick, and they commenced to pray and say, "Jesus, You heal this man." They would be in just exactly the same position Moses was when he got down to the Red Sea and prayed, "Lord God, You divide these waters." The two cases are absolutely parallel. God demands the action of the believer's faith in God. You stretch out your hand and divide the waters.

God has likewise given to every man the measure of faith, and it is for man, as the servant of God, to use the rod that God has given him. In these days there is an attitude of mind that I do not know hardly how to define. It is a mock humility. Rather, it is a false humility. It is a humility that is always hiding behind the Lord and is excusing its own lack of faith by throwing the responsibility over on the Lord. The Word of God, in speaking of this same matter concerning the disciples says, "They departed, and went through the towns, preaching the gospel, and healing every where."

Over and over again throughout the New Testament, the Word of God says, "They healed them, the disciples healed them," etc. You see, they had received something from God. They were as conscious of it as Moses was conscious he had received a rod from the Lord. It was theirs to use. It was theirs to use for all purposes. Peter used the conscious rod of God to heal the man at the beautiful gate. He did not pray. He did not ask God to heal the man, but he commanded him, "In the name of Jesus Christ of Nazareth rise up and walk." And the man obeyed. That was not intercession. It was a command. It was the faith in Peter's soul that brought the result.

Peter used the rod. The rod in this case was the rod of faith. In whose hands was it? In the hands of Peter and John together, and they used that rod of faith. The Word was spoken through Peter. The command was given through him. Unquestionably, John's soul was in it just as much as Peter's was. By faith in His name, by the faith of the disciples, the power of God was made active, and the lame man was healed.

Beloved, the lesson in my soul is this. There is a place of victory and a place of defeat, but there is a hairbreadth line there. It is the place of faith in action. To believe the thing God says and to do the thing that He commands, accepting, as the servant of God, the responsibility God lays upon you. Not interceding as Moses did, but as in Peter's case, through the faith that was in his soul, he commanded the power of God on the man. Suppose Peter had prayed, "Oh Lord, You come and heal this man." It would have been his own acknowledgment of lack of faith to do what Jesus told the disciple to do: heal the sick.

In the story of Saul, in 1 Samuel 10, among other things the prophet Samuel says to him:

"The Spirit of the Lord will come upon thee, and thou shalt prophesy with them, and shalt be turned into another man. And let it be, when these signs are come unto thee, that thou do as occasion serve thee; for God is with thee." (1 Samuel 10:6-7)

The lesson I know God wants us to see tonight is this: He endues a man or woman with the authority of God to accomplish the will of God. The power of God is bestowed upon the man. It is not the man that accomplishes the matter. It is the stretching forth of the hand; the dividing of the waters must be in response to the faith of the man. The man is the instrument. "Thou shalt do as occasion serve thee;

86

for God is with thee." That is, you simply go on about your business, and the power of God is present with you to accomplish the desire of your heart.

Returning to the case of Peter, Peter used the faith of God that was in his soul to restore a man who was born lame, and he was instantly restored.

In the case of Ananias and Sapphira, we see Peter using the same power, by the spoken Word, not to restore a man's limbs, but to bring judgment on a liar. When Ananias lied, the Spirit of God fell on him, and he died as an example of sin. His wife likewise died. "Behold, the feet of them which have buried thy husband are at the door, and shall carry thee out."

Man is a servant of God. Man is an instrument through which God works. The danger line is always around this: The weak men have taken to themselves the glory that belonged to God, and they have said, "We did it." They did not do it. God did it, but the man believed God that it would be done.

How closely we are made co-workers with the Lord, "co-laborers together with Him." It is God's divine purpose to accomplish His will in the world through men. God placed a profound respect upon the Body, "the church, which is his body." I want to show you that.

In the tenth chapter of Acts we have that remarkable response to the prayers of Cornelieus when an angel came to him and said,

"Cornelieus...thy prayers and thine alms are come

up for a memorial before God. And now send men to Joppa, and call for one Simon, whose surname is Peter...he shall tell thee what thou oughtest to do."

The angel came from heaven. He was a direct messenger of God. Yet the angel did not tell Cornelius the way of salvation. Why did the angel instruct Cornelius to send for Peter? Because Peter was a part of the body of Christ, and God ordained that the power of God, with the ministry of Christ, shall be manifest through the Body. Not through angels, but through the Body, "the church, which is his body."

It is, therefore, the duty of the body to use the Spirit of God to accomplish the divine will of God, the purpose of God. With what strength then, with what a consciousness of the dignity of service, Christians ought to go forth! With what a conscious realization that God has bestowed upon you the authority and not only the authority, but the enduement of the Spirit to cause you to believe God and exercise the faith for the will of God to be accomplished.

Is it any wonder that David said,

"What is man, that thou art mindful of him? and the son of man, that thou visitest him? For thou hast made him a little lower than the angels, and hast crowned him with glory and honor. Thou madest him to have dominion over the works of thy hands; thou hast put all things under his feet." (Psalm 8:4-6)

Man and God working together, co-laborers, co-workers. Blessed be God.

9

A TRUMPET CALL

The 13th Chapter of Acts tells us the story of the ordination and sending forth of the apostle Paul, his ordination to the apostleship. Paul never writes of himself as an apostle until after the 13th chapter of Acts. He had been an evangelist and teacher for thirteen years when the 13th of Acts was written, and the ordination that took place is recorded there. Men who have a real call are not afraid of apprenticeships.

There is a growing up in experience in the ministry. When Paul started out in the ministry he was definitely called of God and was assured of God through Ananias that it would not be an easy service but a terrific one, for God said to Ananias:

"Arise and go into the street which is called Straight, and inquire in the house of Judas for one called Saul of Tarsus for, behold, he prayeth; He is a chosen vessel unto me, to bear my Name before the Gentiles, and kings, and the children of Israel: For I will show him how great things he must suffer for my Name's sake." (See Acts 9:11, 15-16)

That is what Jesus Christ, the crucified and glorified Son of God told Ananias to say to the Apostle Paul. He was not going to live in a holy ecstasy and wear a beautiful halo, and have a heavenly time and ride in a limousine. He was going to have a drastic time, a desperate struggle, a terrific experience. And no man in Biblical history ever had more dreadful things to endure than the Apostle Paul. He gives a list in his letter to the Corinthians of the things he had endured.

"Of the Jews five times received I forty stripes save one. Thrice I was beaten with rods. Once was I stoned, thrice I suffered shipwreck, a night and a day have I been in the deep; in journeyings often, in perils of waters, in perils of robbers, in perils by mine own countrymen, in perils by the heathen, in perils in the city, in perils in the wilderness, in perils in the sea, in perils among false brethren. In weariness and painfulness, in watchings often, in hunger and thirst in fastings often, in cold and nakedness." (2 Corinthians 11:24-27)

They stripped him of his clothing, and the executioner lashed him with an awful scourge, until bleeding and lacerated and broken, he fell helpless, and unconscious and insensible; then they doused him with a bucket of salt water to keep the maggots off, and threw him into a cell to recover. That was the price of apostleship. That was the "price" of the call of God and His service. But God said, "They shall bear my Name before the Gentiles and kings, and the children of Israel." He qualified as God's messenger.

Beloved, we have lost the character of

consecration here manifested. God is trying to restore it in our day. He has not been able to make much progress with the average preacher on that line. "Mrs. So-and-So said so-and-so, and I am just not going to take it." That is the kind of preacher, with another kind of call, not the heaven call, not the God call, not the death call if necessary. That is not the kind the Apostle Paul had.

Do you want to know why God poured out His Spirit in South Africa like He did no where else in the world? There was a reason. This example will illustrate. We had one hundred and twenty-five men out on the field at one time. We were a very young institution; were not known in the world. South Africa is seven thousand miles from any European country. It is ten thousand miles by way of England to the United States. Our finances got so low under the awful assault we were compelled to endure, that there came a time I could not even mail to these workers at the end of the month a $10 bill. It got so I could not send them $2. The situation was desperate. What was I to do? Under these circumstances I did not want to take the responsibility of leaving men and their families on the frontier without real knowledge of what the conditions were.

Some of us at headquarters sold our clothes in some cases, sold certain pieces of furniture out of the house, sold anything we could sell, to bring those hundred and twenty-five workers off the field for a conference.

One night in the progress of the conference I was invited by a committee to leave the room for a minute or two. The conference wanted to have a word by themselves. So I stepped out to a restaurant for a cup of coffee, and came back. When I came in I found they had rearranged the chairs in an oval, with a little table at one end, and on the table was the bread and the wine. Old Father Van der Wall, speaking for the company said, "Brother Lake, during Your absence we have come to a conclusion; we have made our decision. We want you to serve the Lord's supper. We are going back to our fields. We are going back if we have to walk back. We are going back if we have to starve. We are going back if our wives die. We are going back if our children die. We are going back if we die ourselves. We have but one request. If we die, we want you to come and bury us."

The next year I buried twelve men, sixteen wives and children. In my judgment not one of the twelve, if they had had a few of things a white man needs to eat but what might have lived. Friends, when you want to find out why the power of God came down from heaven in South Africa like it never came down before since the times of the apostles, there is your answer.

Jesus Christ put the spirit of martyrdom in the ministry. Jesus instituted his ministry with a pledge unto death. When He was with the disciples on the last night He took the cup, "when He drank, saying." Beloved, the SAYING was the significant thing. It was Jesus Christ's pledge to the twelve who stood with Him, "This cup is the New Testament in my blood." Then He said, "Drink ye all of it."

Friends, those who were there and drank to that pledge, of Jesus Christ, entered into the same covenant and purpose that He did. That is what all pledges mean. Men have pledged themselves in the wine cup from time immemorial. Generals have pledged their armies unto death. It has been a custom in the race. Jesus Christ sanctified it to the Church forever, bless God.

"My blood in the New Testament." "Drink ye all of it." Let us become one. Let us become one in our purpose to die for the world. Your blood and Mine, together. "My blood in the New Testament." It is my demand from you. It is your high privilege. Dear friends, there is not an authentic history that can tell us whether any one of them died a natural death. We know that at least nine of them were martyrs, possibly all. Peter died on a cross, James was beheaded, for Thomas they did not even wait to make a cross: they nailed him to an olive tree. John was sentenced to be executed at Ephesus by putting him in a cauldron of boiling oil. God delivered him, and his executioners refused to repeat the operation, and he was banished to the Isle of Patmos. John thought so little about it that he never even tells of the incident. He says, "I was in the Isle called Patmos, for the Word of God, and for the testimony of Jesus Christ." That was explanation enough. He had committed himself to

Jesus Christ for life or death.

Friends, the group of missionaries that followed me went without food, and went without clothes, and once when one of my preachers was sunstruck, and had wandered away, I tracked him by the blood marks of his feet. Another time I was hunting for one of my missionaries, a young Englishman, 22 years of age. He had come from a line of Church of England preachers for five hundred years. When I arrived at the native village the old native chief said, "He is not here. He went over the mountains, and you know, Mr., he is a white man and he has not learned to walk bare footed."

That is the kind of consecration that established Pentecost in South Africa. That is the reason we have a hundred thousand native Christians in South Africa. That is the reason we have 1250 native preachers. That is the reason we have 350 white Churches in South Africa. That is the reason that today we are the most rapid growing Church in South Africa.

I am not persuading you, dear friends, by holding out a hope that the way is going to be easy. I am calling you in the Name of Jesus Christ, you dear ones who expect to be ordained to the Gospel of Jesus Christ tonight, take the route that Jesus took, the route the apostles took, the route that the early Church took, the victory route, whether by life or death. Historians declare, "The blood of the martyrs was the seed of the Church" (Tertullian, 197 AD). Beloved, that is what the difficulty is in our day: we have so little seed. The Church needs more martyr blood.

If I were pledging men and women to the Gospel of the Son of God, as I am endeavoring to do tonight, it would not be to have a nice Church and harmonious surroundings, and a sweet do nothing time. I would invite them to be ready to die. That was the spirit of early Methodism. John Wesley established a heroic call. He demanded every preacher to be "ready to pray, ready to preach, ready to die." That is always the spirit of Christianity. When there is any other spirit that comes into the Church, it is not the spirit of Christianity. It is a foreign spirit. It is a sissified substitute.

I lived on corn meal mush many a period with my family, and we did not growl, and I preached to thousands of people, not colored people, but white people. My missionaries were on the field existing on corn meal mush, I could not eat pie. My heart was joined to them. That is the reason we never had splits in our work in South Africa. One country where Pentecost never split. The split business began to develop years afterward, when pumpkin pie eating Pentecostal missionaries began infesting the country. Men who are ready to die for the Son of God do not split. They do not holler the first time they get the stomach ache. Bud Robinson tells a story of himself. He went to preach in the southern mountains. It was the first time in his life that no one invited him to go home and eat with them. So he slept on the floor, and the next night, and the next night. After five days and five nights had passed, and his stomach began to growl for food terribly, every once in a while he would stop and say, "Lay down, you brute" and he went on with his sermon. That is what won. That is what will win every time. That is what we need today. We need men who are willing to get off the highway. When I started to preach the gospel I walked twenty miles on Sunday morning to my service and walked home twenty miles in the night when I got through. I did it for years, for Jesus and souls.

In early Methodism an old local preacher would start Saturday and walk all night, and then walk all night Sunday night to get back to his work. It was the common custom. Peter Cartwright preached for sixty dollars per year and baptized ten thousand converts.

Friends, we talk about consecration, and we preach about consecration, but that is the kind of consecration that my heart is asking for tonight. That is the kind of consecration that will get answers from heaven. That is the kind God will honor. That is the consecration to which I would pledge Pentecost. I would strip Pentecost of its frills and fall-de-ralls. Jesus Christ, through the Holy Ghost, calls us tonight not to an earthly mansion and a ten thousand dollar motor car, but to put our lives, body and soul and spirit, on the altar of service. All hail! Ye who are ready to die for Christ and this glorious Pentecostal Gospel, we salute you. You are brothers with us and with your Lord.

10

SCIENCE OF HEALING

"In Him was life, and life was the light of men."
—John 1:4

There is a difference between Christianity and philosophy. (I presume some folks are inquiring why it is that there is always that key note in my addresses.)

God gave me the privilege of living in the heart of philosophic South Africa, where we have one million five hundred thousand, who are ministered to by Buddhist, and Brahman priests. Every imaginable cult has its representatives there. I was amazed to discover that the whites were gradually assimilating the philosophy of the East, just as we Westerners are assimilating the philosophy of the East, and have been doing so for a long time.

When you take the philosophies, Christian Science, New Thought, and Unity today and examine them, you discover they are the same old philosophies of India, Egypt and China from time immemorial.

The difference between philosophy and religion, particularly the religion of Jesus Christ, is in the words I have quoted from the Scriptures, "In Him was Life, and the life was the light of men." Philosophy is light. It is the best light the individual possessed who framed the philosophy. But it is not a LIFE GIVER.

But from the soul of Jesus there breathed holy, living life of God, that comes into the nature of man, quickens him by its power, and by the grace of God he has the life of Jesus in him, eternal life. Many of the ancient philosophies have a marvelous light. One of the Indian philosophies, Bavgad, was written five hundred years before Isaiah. In it they predicted the coming of a Son of God, a Redeemer, who was to come and redeem mankind.

Buddha presented his philosophy five hundred years before Jesus. Pathergoris wrote four thousand years before Jesus Christ. In each one of them you will find many of the teachings of Jesus. The teachings of Jesus were not unique in that they were all new. They were new because they contained something that none of the rest possessed. It was the divine content in the word of Jesus Christ that gave His teachings their distinguishing feature from the other philosophies. That content (element) is the LIFE of God. "In Him was LIFE, and the LIFE was the light of men."

Beloved, the real Christian, and the real Christian Church, undertakes to bring to mankind the life of the Lord Jesus, knowing that when the LIFE of Jesus comes, the light of civilization and Christianity will follow, but the LIFE is the first thing.

As men traveled from God, and as the world traveled from God, men naturally fell into their own consciousness and soul states, and proceeded in the common way of the world to endeavor to bless the world through LIGHT. But LIGHT never saved a world. Light will never save the world. There must be a divine content from on high that comes to the soul to enrich it and to empower it, to illuminate it, and to glorify it, and more, to deify it! For God's purpose through Jesus Christ is to deify the natures of men, and thus forever make them like unto, not only in their outward appearance and habits of life, but in nature and substance and content, in spirit and soul and body, LIKE THE SON OF GOD.

Jesus never intended Christians to be an imitation. They were to be bone of His bone, and blood of His blood, and flesh of His flesh, and soul of His soul, and spirit of His Spirit. In this He becomes the Son of God, and a Redeemer forever.

In my youth I took a course in medicine. I never practiced medicine, for I abandoned the whole subject a few months before the time of my graduation, when it came to the piece where diagnosis became the general subject for examination. It was then that I discovered that the whole subject of diagnosis was very largely a matter of guesswork, and it so remains.

Consequently, throughout my life, there has remained in me somewhat of the spirit of investigation. It has never been easy to accept things readily, until my soul stepped out inch by inch and proved them for myself.

When I approached the matter of baptism, I did so with great care, but I approached it as a hungry soul; my heart was hungry for God, and one day the Spirit of the Lord came upon me. God flooded my life and baptized me in His Holy Spirit. Then began in my heart a new and powerful working of God, which has gone on for fifteen years, until Christ has become to my soul a divine reality.

Having had former acknowledgment as a medical student, it is still my privilege to attend a medical clinic, which I frequently do. I submitted myself at one time to a series of experiments. It was not sufficient to know that God did things, I had to know HOW God accomplished these things.

So, when I returned from Africa, at one time I visited at the John Hopkins institution, and submitted myself for this series of experiments.

First, they attached to my head an instrument to record the vibrations of the brain. This instrument had an indicator that would mark according to the vibrations of the mind. I began by repeating soothing things, like the Twenty-third Psalm; then I repeated the Thirty-seventh Psalm and then the thirty-fifth chapter of Isaiah, the ninety-first Psalm; and Paul's address before Agrippa. Then, I went into secular literature, and I repeated the Charge of the Light Brigade, Poe's Raven, with a prayer in my heart that somehow God would connect my soul in the Holy Ghost. My difficulty was that while this was going on I could not keep the Spirit from coming upon me, and when I got through with Poe's Raven, they said, "You are a phenomenon. You have a wider mental range than any human being we have ever seen." But it was this, that the Spirit of God kept coming upon me in degree, so I could feel the moving of the Spirit within me.

But I prayed in my heart, "Lord God, if you will only let the Spirit of God come like the lightnings of God upon my soul for two seconds, I know something is going to happen that these men never saw before."

So I closed the last lines. All at once the Spirit of God struck me in a burst of praise and tongues, and the old indicator on the instrument went to the end of the rod and I haven't the least idea how much further it would have gone if there had been an indicator to record it. The instructors said, "We have never seen anything like it!" I replied, "Brethren, it is the Holy Ghost!"

Now in order to get the force of what I want to tell you in this next experiment is something of the processes of digestion. I want to explain the assimilating power of your nature, your capacity to assimilate God and take the life of God into your being, and keep it in your being. I am not talking to you about what I believe. I am talking about what I know.

For twenty-five years God has kept me so that sickness, nor the devil, were able to touch me, from the day that I saw in the ninety-first Psalm a man's privilege of entering into God, not only for healing, but HEALTH, and having God and the life of God in every fiber of his being.

Scientists tell us that in a single inch of a man's skin there are one million, five-hundred thousand cells. They have almost doubled that statement now. But be that as it may, I want you to see that the whole structure of man's life is one wonderful cellular structure. Your body, your brain, your bone is just one great cellular structure.

In the process of digestion it is something like this. The food we eat is reduced to vegetable lymph before it is absorbed by the body. But no scientist in the world has ever been able to satisfactorily explain what it is that changes the lymph and makes it life. Something happens when it is in the body that changes it to life.

I want to tell you what grew up in my soul, and how I proved the fact. I could feel sometimes in the attitude of prayer, just as you have felt hundreds of times, the impulse of the Spirit moving down through your brain and your person to the end of your fingers just little impulses of God's presence in your life. And I have said, "If there was an instrument powerful enough I believe men could see the action of the brain cells, and see what took place."

Here is the secret of digestion. When from the spirit of man, and through the spirit of man there is being imparted to every cell of your body waves of light, waves of life. It is the movement of your spirit.

Spirit impulses passing from the cortex cells of the brain to the very end of your fingers and toes, to every cell of your body. And when they touch that vegetable lymph it is transformed into life. That is common transmutation.

In the material world you can dissolve zinc and attach a wire, and transmit it to the other end of the wire. They dissolve that zinc, and the battery at the one end, and transmit the zinc to the other end of the wire, where it is deposited. How is it done? There is a process of transmutation. That is what it is called. There is change from one form to another.

My brother, you listen to me, if that is not true in the spiritual world, there is no such thing as divine LIFE. There is no such thing as salvation through the Son of God. For that which is soulish must be transformed by the Spirit of God in us, until it becomes spiritual, until it is of God. Jesus sat with His disciples and ate with them, both bread and fish. He went to the mount and ascended before them to Glory. What happened to the fish and bread that He ate? I tell you there is a transmutation. That which is natural becomes spiritual. That which was natural is changed by the power of God into the life of God, into the nature of God, into the substance of God, into the glory of God.

So when I returned to this country this time, I submitted myself for this experiment. They attached to my head a powerful instrument that could take some kind of picture one after another, in order to see, if possible, what the action of the brain cells would be. Then I repeated things that were soothing and calculated to reduce the action of the cortex cells to their lowest possible action. Then I went on into the scriptures to the better and richer things, until I came to the first of John, and as I began to recite that, and the fires of God began to burn in my heart, presently once again the Spirit of God came upon me, and the man who was at my back touched me. It was a signal to keep that poise until one after another could look through the instrument. And finally when I let go, and the Spirit subsided, they said, "Why man, we cannot understand this thing, but the cortex cells extended so that we can hardly imagine it possible to a human brain."

Oh, I'll tell you, when you pray, something is happening in you. It is not a myth. It is the action of God. It is scientific that the almighty God comes into the soul, takes possession of the brain, lives in the cortex cells, and when you will or wish, either consciously or unconsciously, the fire of God, the power of God, that life of God, that nature of God, throbs through your nerves, down through your person into every cell of your being, into every million five-hundred thousand cells in every square inch of your skin, and they are alive with God.

Men have treated the Gospel of Jesus Christ as though it were a sentiment and foolishness. Men who posed as being wise, have scorned the simple things that were taking place every day. But I want to tell you that no dear old mother ever knelt before the Throne of God, and raised her heart to heaven without demonstrating the finest process of the divine wireless transmission of God that ever was produced.

In these days they are now able to transmit by wireless from six to seven thousand miles, and even twelve thousand miles recently (1920). Once again they have been able to demonstrate that in one-tenth of a second they can transmit the first section of thought twelve thousand miles. Think of it! There is practically no such thing as time.

Beloved, the very instant your soul moves with your heart cries, that yearning of your soul, it registers in the soul of Jesus Christ, and the answer comes back.

I said to them, Gentlemen, I want you to see one more thing. You go down in your hospital and bring a man who has inflammation in the bone. So they brought up a man with inflammation in the bone. I said, "You take your instrument, and attach it to that fellow's leg, but you leave enough space to get my hand on his leg you can have it attached on both sides." So when the thing was all ready, I put my hand on that man's shin, and I prayed just like Mother Etter prays. No strange prayer, but the cry of my heart to God. I said, "God, kill this devilish business by the power of God, let it live in him, let it move in him." Then I said, "Gentlemen, what is taking place?" They replied, "Every cell responds." All there is to it is that the life of God comes back into the part that is afflicted, and right away the blood flows in, and the work is done.

My soul has grown tired long ago of men treating the whole subject of Christianity as though it were child's play. We have our physical sciences, we have our psychological sciences, the action of the mind, taught in the great schools of the land, but there is something greater. One of these days there is going to be a new chair. It will be the chair of pneumatology, the science of spirit, by which men will undertake to discover the laws of God. And by the grace of God, men shall know that God is alive, and the living Spirit of God is no dream.

In my healing rooms at Spokane, there came one day a dear woman whose name is Lamphear. She is the wife of a merchant in the city. She had fallen down a stairs, causing a prolapses of the bowels and stomach. She had been an invalid for eleven years. On top of that she had become tubercular. On top of that the poor thing developed inflammatory rheumatism, until she was terribly deformed. She was going to die. The doctors said there was nothing they could do for her. They advised that she be taken to Hot Lake, Oregon, and perhaps that would do her some good. So they put her in hot baths there and she suffered just as much as ever. So they thought they would try super-heated baths. They put her in water hotter than any human being had ever been in before. The results was that instead of having any healing effect, the left leg developed an abnormal growth, and it became three inches shorter than the other leg. It is a simple condition of sarcoma. The foot became an inch longer. She came away from the institution worse than when she went. She got as far as Portland. Her parents were living in the Dalles. She wanted to see her parents before she died. Her husband carried her in his arms onto the ship. As he did so, a Pentecostal missionary stepped up and said, "Dear woman, we understand now why God told us to take this boat. The Lord told us last night to take the eight o'clock boat for The Dalles." He had called up on the telephone and found the fare was $1.80, and as that was all the money they had, they went without their breakfast so as to be able to take the boat.

As she lay crying with her suffering, they said, "When we get to The Dalles, we will pray for you." (They were timid folks.) Eventually they reached The Dalles and went to a hotel. The two knelt to pray for her. She says as they prayed and put their hands on her knees, their hands became illuminated until they looked like the hands of Jesus, their faces looked like the face of Jesus, and she was afraid. But something happened. The pain went out of her.

Strangely, she retained the tuberculosis and the struggle for breath. The leg remained the same length.When she examined herself, she was surprised that it was not shorter. She said, "Pray again that the Lord may make it the same length as the other," but the poor missionary was staggered. He said, "Dear

Sister, the pain is gone. You be satisfied and give praise to God."

So she went on three and a half years coughing her lungs out and with her leg longer than the other. One day she came to the healing rooms and was ministered to by Mr. Westwood, and she felt relieved. She said, "Mr. Westwood, I saw breath clear down into my stomach." He said, "I'll pray for that." "But," she said, "the man told me I should be satisfied that the pain was gone." Mr. Westwood said, "He had not grown up in God yet." Mr. Westwood put his hands on that lump and prayed, and God Almighty dissolved that lump of bone, and that leg shortened at the rate of one inch a day, and she wears shoes like anyone else.

There is a difference between healing and miracles. Healing is the restoration of diseased tissue, but miracle is a creative action of the Spirit of God in a man's life. And the salvation of a soul is a divine miracle of God. Every time Christ speaks the word of LIFE to a man's heart there is a divine creative miracle of God in him, and he is a new man in Christ Jesus.

One day I sat in Los Angeles talking to old father Seymour. I told him of an incident in the life of Elias Letwaba, one of our native preachers, who lived in the native country. I came to his home, and his wife said, "He is not home. A little baby is hurt, and he is over praying for it." So we went over and got down on our knees and crawled into the native hut. I saw he was kneeling in a corner by the dying child. I said, "Letwaba, it is me. What is the matter with the child?" He told me that it had hurt its neck. I examined it and saw that the baby's neck is broken, and I said to Letwaba, "Why, Letwaba, the baby's neck is broken." I did not have faith for a broken neck, but poor old Letwaba did not know the difference, and I saw he did not understand; but he discerned the spirit of doubt in my soul. I said to myself, "I am not going to interfere with his faith. He will just feel the doubt and all the old traditional things I ever learned, so I will go out" and I did. I went out and sat in another hut and kept on praying. I went to bed at one o'clock at three o'clock Letwaba came in. I said, "Well, Letwaba how about the baby?" He looked at me lovingly and sweetly and said, "Why brother, the baby is all well." I said, "The baby is well! Take me to the baby at once." I went to the baby and took the little black thing on my arm, and I came out and prayed, "Lord, take every cursed thing out of my soul that keeps me from believing the Lord Jesus Christ."

In my meeting in Spokane is a dear man who told us he was dying of pellagra. He came from Dallas, Texas, to sister Etter's meetings. Apparently, he died on the train and they laid his body at the station house and covered him with some gunny sacks, but, they discovered in the morning he was still alive. So they carried him to Mother Etter's meetings and she came down off the platform and prayed for him. That man is living, and has been preaching the gospel for seven years at Spokane.

Why, there is more science in the Son of God in five minutes than the ignorant old world ever knew. "In HIM was LIFE, and the LIFE as the light of men." The LIFE of God is that which the mind of men, and the keenest of them, never knew, and never discovered. "The world through wisdom knew not God." They could not discern His death nor understand the marvels of His life, until the Lord Jesus came and lived and died and entered into Hades and destroyed the powers of darkness and liberated the souls of men; liberated them from the chains of darkness and came forth into the world to speak God's word and reveal God's power and show God's nature. And by the grace of God, we have been privileged to enter into the nature of Jesus, and the fires of God burn in his soul like they burned in the soul of Jesus. The scientific world has been startled by one of the English scientists who has come forward with a formula for transmuting the grosser metals into gold. It did not work. Years ago this knowledge was known to the world, but somehow it disappeared from the world. Recently men again have attempted to change lead, silver and iron, transmuting them into gold.

Beloved, that is the thing that Jesus Christ has been doing all the time. It is as old as Christianity, and as old as the Son of God. He has been coming to the hearts of men, taking the old base conditions of the nature, and in the mighty action of the Holy Ghost, they have been changed into pure gold of God. If there never was another blessing that came to the world through Pentecost but this one, all the price that men could pay would be as nothing for it. For I want to tell you there has been more real divine researching by the Holy Ghost into the nature of God and the nature of men in these last fifteen years that there ever was in the whole world. When anyone comes to me with the statement that there is nothing in the Holy Ghost but a psychological manifestation, I say, "Brother, sister, come with me and see the gems of God and the beautiful gold that has come out of the dross and the dirty lives, and then you will know."

In my assembly at Spokane is a dear little woman who was totally blind for nine years. She had little teaching along the line of faith in God. She sat one day with her group of six children to discover that the dirty brute of a husband had abandoned her. A debased human being is capable of things that no beast will do, for a beast will care for its own. You can imagine what that little heart was like. She was broken and bruised and bleeding. She gathered her children around her and began to pray. They were sitting on their front porch. Presently the little one got up and said, "Oh, Mama, there is a man coming up the path, and he looks like Jesus. Oh, Mama, there is blood on His hands and blood on His feet!" And the children were frightened and ran around the corner of the house. After a while the biggest one looked around the corner and said, "Why, Mama, He is laying His hands on your eyes!" And just then her blind eyes opened.

And Beloved, if we could have seen the reason, we would have seen that there were some Christians at Zion City or some other place who were praying the power of God on a hungry world, and Jesus Christ in His search, rushed into her life and sent her forth to praise God and teach the Gospel of Jesus.

I would not have missed my life in Africa for anything. It put me up against some of the real problems. I sat upon the Mount of Sources one night, and I counted eleven hundred native villages within the range of my eyes. I could see the color of the grass on the mountains sixty miles away. I could see the mountains one hundred and fifty miles away. Then I began to figure, and I said, "Within the range of my eyes there lives at least ten million native people. They've never heard the name of Jesus." In the whole land there are at least one hundred million people, perhaps two hundred million. They are being born every day at a tremendous rate. Do you know there are more heathen born every day than are Christianized in fifty years? When are we going to catch up by our present method of building schools and teaching them to read? Never! I tell you it will never come that way. It has got to come from heaven by the power of God, by an outpouring of the Holy Ghost.

That is the reason that in my heart I rejoice in the blessed promise. "In the last days," saith God, "I will pour out my Spirit upon all flesh." And every last one of the two hundred million poor black people are going to hear and know of the Lord Jesus Christ. And beloved, I would rather have a place in the kingdom of God to pray that thing into existence, and to pray the power of God upon them, than anything else in the world.

Africa is said to be the first settled country in the world, and we believe it is six thousand years old. Africa has been settled for five thousand years. Two hundred to four hundred million have died every century. Split the difference, and say that three hundred million have died every year for five thousand years.

I began to pray. I said, "Has God no interest in these people, and if He has an interest, why is not something done for them? What is the matter with God?" My heart was breaking under the burden of it. I said, "God, there is an explanation somewhere. What is it, Lord? Tell me about this thing."

After a while the Spirit said, "The Church which is His Body," and I knew that was God's answer. I said, "Yes, the church should have sent missionaries and built schools and done this and that." The Church, which is His body. And I sat and listened to that voice repeat that sentence for a half hour. I said, "My God, my soul begins to see. The Church is the generating power of God in the world; the Church has been negligent in one thing. She has not prayed the power of God out of heaven."

Then I saw that which has become a conviction in my soul from that day. There never was a soul born to God in the whole earth at any time until some soul in the world got hold of the living Spirit of God and generated that Spirit in saving grace and creative virtue, until it took possession of a soul, no difference if it was a million miles away.

When I try to induce men to forget their little squabbles and little differences and go praying, it is because my soul feels the burden of it. Mother Etter has been like a marshal for fifty years. The sick have been healed, people have been converted and blessed. But beloved, when I heard of Brother Brooks shutting himself up night and day to pray the power of God on a world, I said, "That is where she gets her fire; and from where it comes to my soul; that is from where it comes to every other soul."

Look how beautifully this hall is lighted. Do you know the world lived in darkness for five thousand years and they had no way of lighting a place except by torches. But there was just as much electricity five thousand years ago as there is today. Somebody found how to handle it, discovered the laws that govern it. To this day there is not a man who can tell us what electricity is, or what its substance is. We know we can control it this way and guide it that way, and make it do this and that, but what it is, nobody can tell us. But down somewhere on the river there is a thing that is called a dynamo, and its draws the electricity out of the air, and transmits it over the wires, and these days they are even sending it wireless.

Do you know what prayer is? It is not begging God for this and that. The first thing we have to do is to get you beggars to quit begging until a little faith moves in your souls. PRAYER is God's divine dynamo. The spirit of man is God's divine dynamo. When you go to pray, that spirit of yours gets into motion, not ten thousand revolutions or one hundred thousand. The voltage of heaven comes to your heart, and it flows from your hands, it burns into the souls of men, and God Almighty moves on their behalf.

Over in Indiana some years ago was a farmer who used to be a friend of Brother Fockler and myself. His son had been in South America, had a dreadful case of typhoid fever, had no proper nursing and the result was a great fever sore developed until it was seven inches in diameter. The whole abdomen became grown up with proud flesh, one layer on top of another layer, until there were five layers. The nurse would lift up those layers and wash then with an antiseptic to keep the maggots out of it. When he exposed the body for me to pray for him, I had never seen anything like that before. I was shocked. As I went to pray for him, I spread my fingers out over that sore. I prayed, "God, in the name of Jesus Christ, blast this curse of hell and burn it up by the power of God." Then I took the train and came back. The next day I received a telegram saying, "Lake, the most unusual thing has happened. An hour after you left the whole print of your hand was burned into that

116

thing a quarter of an inch deep, and it is there yet."

You talk about the voltage of heaven and the power of God. Why, there is lightning in the soul of Jesus. The lightnings of Jesus heal men by its touch, sin dissolves, disease flees when the power of God approaches.

And yet, we are quibbling and wondering if Jesus Christ is big enough for our need. Let's take the bars down. Let God come into your life. And in the name of Jesus your heart will not be satisfied with an empty Pentecost, but the light of God and the lightnings of Jesus will flood your life. Amen!

11

CHRISTIAN CONSCIOUSNESS

There is a wonderful single word that expresses what God is trying to develop in us. That word is, consciousness. I love it. It is an amazing word. Consciousness means, that which the soul knows. Not that which you believe, or that which you have an existent faith for, or that which you hope, but that which the soul has proven, which the soul knows, upon which the soul rests, the thing, bless God, which has become concrete in your life.

Consequently God's purpose, and the purpose of real religion, is to create in the nature of man a consciousness of God. And that church which will succeed in creating the highest degree of consciousness of God in the soul of men, will live longest in the world. And the only mode of possibility of perpetuating a church in the world forever is to bring into the souls of the people the full measure of the consciousness of God that Jesus Christ enjoys.

It is a good thing, not only to be good, but to know WHY you are good. It is not only a good thing to be an American, but to know WHY you are an American. It is a good thing, not only to be a Christian but to know WHY you are a Christian, and to know why Christian consciousness is superior to every other known consciousness.

I want to declare that Christianity stands superior to every other form of religion under the heavens and in the whole earth; that no other religion under the heavens has the same consciousness of God or the same means of producing a consciousness of God, that Christianity possesses.

In 1893 in this city, was the great Chicago World's Fair. Among the features of the fair was a Congress on Religions. All the religions of the world were invited to send their representatives and present their peculiar religion for the good of all. Many regarded it as a great calamity that the varied forms of Eastern Philosophy should thus be introduced into this country. I never felt that way. I have always felt that if Christianity could not demonstrate her superiority over every other religion, then Christianity has not the place and power that Jesus Christ said Christianity had in the world.

But the result of that Congress of Religions was that Christianity was so poorly presented, that the Indian Philosophers ran away with the whole thing, and in the minds of thousands who listened, it left a belief that their knowledge of God, and God's laws, and the laws of life were greater than the Christian possessed.

And, fellow Christians, there began in my soul a prayer that Almighty God would reveal in my soul what the real secret of real Christianity is, in order that, in this world, Christians might become kings and priests, and demonstrate the superiority of the religion of the Son of God, beyond that of every other in the whole earth.

In later years I went to South Africa. It was at a time of peculiar interest in South African history, just following the Boer War. The great industry there is mining. One fourth of the gold of the world comes from Johannesburg and vicinity. The diamonds of the world come from South Africa, and the United States is the greatest diamond market of the world.

When the Boer War came on, the native people became so frightened over war between white men, that after the war was over and settled, they could not coax them back to open the mines. The result was, that in order to get the industries established again, they had to send to China and get two-hundred thousand Chinese, and put them to work to open the shops and mines, and all the other industries. These Chinese came in real colonies. Some were followers of Confucius, some were Buddhists, some where Brahmans, some represented this form, and some that form of philosophy. They brought their priests, and their priests ministered unto them.

At the same time there were in South Africa, one and a half million East Indians. These represented all the cults of India. They made complaints that they were not being properly cared for, and the British government sent to India and imported a great company of Buddhist priests, and Brahman priests, and Yogi priests, and all the rest of them, and they came to South Africa to assist their own people.

I had a Jewish friend, Rabbi Hertz, who became famous as a great Rabbi, because of his influence for the British, during the war. There was also a Roman Catholic priest, Father Bryant, a wonderful man. I listened to Dr. Hertz give a series of lectures on the Psalms of David, which I regard as the finest of that character I had ever heard.

One day he said, "Did it ever occur to you what an amazing Congress of Religions we have in this country? It would put the one in Chicago, in 1893, in the shade." I said, "I have thought of it, but do not have sufficient acquaintance among these other men to undertake it, but would gladly give a helping hand." So it was eventually brought to pass.

We gathered once a week. They sat on the floor all night, Eastern fashion, a priest with his interpreter, and we gave the individual a whole night if he wanted it, or two nights if he wanted it, or as long as he wanted, to tell out the very secret of his soul, to show the very best he could, the very depth of his peculiar religion, and the consciousness of God it produced. It was not the details of his religion we sought, but the soul of it, and the consciousness it possessed. We listened to the Indian Buddhist priest one night, and the Chinese Buddhist priest the next night, and it went on. Eventually it came to the night that Dr. Hertz, the Jewish Rabbi, was to give the secret of the Jewish religion, and tell out the whole of God that the Jewish religion revealed, and the consciousness of God that was produced by the Mosaic and the prophetic teachings.

Did you ever stop to think that in all religious history, the Jewish prophets knew more of God than all the Philosophers of earth combined? They superseded all others of the ancients in knowledge of God, His ways and power. They gave to their day and generation such a revelation of God as the world had never known. Stop and think of the wonders of God that the Old Testament revealed. Think of the marvels, that it seems would stagger the very soul of modern Christianity.

When the Israelites were traveling over the deserts, God arrested the processes of decay in their very shoes and clothing, and they wore them continually for forty years. Think of the marvel of it, the arrest of the process of decay! And then someone wonders if it is possible to arrest the process of decay in a man's life. Yes, it is, bless God! Jesus Christ arrested the process of death by the power of God, through the introduction of the life and the Spirit of life in Jesus Christ, giving man eternal life.

Think again of the old prophet who, when they had lost the ax in the water, and came to him in their distress, and he takes a stick and holds it in his hands. What for? Until that stick became magnetized by the Spirit and power of God. And when he threw it in the water, the ax arose and came to the stick. Think again of the prophet when he was called to the dying boy. He said to his servant, "Take this staff," the staff that he carried, "go ahead of me, lay it on the child." What for? Because he carried that staff next to his God anointed hands until the staff itself became impregnated with the life and power of God. So the servant went ahead, and there was enough of God in that staff to keep the life there, and the spirit there, until he arrived and called the child to life by the power of God.

Later they were burying a man, and in their haste they opened the grave of Elisha, and when the dead man touched his old God-filled bones, he became alive. There was enough of God in the old bones to quicken him into life again. Bless God!

You say, "Well, how can Christianity demonstrate anything further than that?" When I listened to Dr. Hertz my heart asked, "Dear God, when I get my turn to reveal what Christianity is, what am I going to say that is going to reveal Christianity as superior to the Jewish dispensation, and the consciousness of God that it produced in the souls of the prophets?"

From eight o'clock at night until four thirty, Dr. Hertz poured out his soul in a wondrous stream of God revelation, such as my soul had never heard. In the morning as I started for home I prayed, "God, in the name of Jesus, when it comes next Thursday night, and it is my turn to show forth Jesus Christ, what am I going to say to surmount the revelation of God that he gave?" I had searched Christian literature for it. I had searched the libraries of the world. I could not find it in the writings of the old Christian Fathers. I searched the Word of God for it. I saw flashes of it, but somehow it would not frame in my soul. I decided there was only one way. I gave myself to fasting and prayer and waiting on God. And one day, in the quiet, God told me that secret.

And from that day my heart rested in the new vision of Jesus Christ, and a new revelation of the real divinity of Christianity came to my heart.

So it came my turn and I sat down and reviewed for hours, with care, step by step, the consciousness that the philosophers and priests had shown as belonging to their respective religions, and finally the wonderful consciousness that Dr. Hertz had shown as belonging to the Mosaic dispensation.

Oh, bless God, there is a secret in Jesus Christ. Christianity is all supernatural, every bit of it. The philosophers are natural. The Mosaic dispensation and its revelation was supernatural, but its revelation did not have the high degree of overcoming consciousness that belongs to Christianity. Yet, you can go around the world, and you will not find one in a hundred thousand that can tell what the real secret of Christianity is, which makes it superior to all other religions.

You say, "It is the Holy Ghost." Well, the prophets had the Holy Ghost. There is no more marvelous record given than the Old Testament records. When Moses wanted mechanics and workmen, the Lord called a man by name and said, "I have placed the

Spirit of God in wisdom, and in understanding, and in knowledge, and in all manner of cunning works, to work in gold, and in silver, and in brass, and in cutting of stones, to set them, and in carving of timber, to work all manner of workmanship." That is the way they learned their trade.

Later, they were making preparations for the building of Solomon's temple. That temple is one of the seven wonders of the world. Did you ever stop to think of where the plans came from, or how they got them? Old David tells us that God gave him the plans of the temple in writing; "while the Spirit of God was upon me in writing," and he wrote the details of it. He put these details down with such accuracy that they prepared the temple in the mountains, and when they came to put it together, there was no sound of a hammer. Every piece fit into place. What a wonderful moving of God! What a wonderful presence of God! Talk about the glory of God! Why, when Moses came down from the mountain, his face shown or radiated with the glory of God so intensely that the people were afraid of him, and he was compelled to wear a veil until the anointing had somewhat left his soul.

But, beloved, Christianity is more than that. Paul declares that the glory of Moses' face was superseded. I said a moment ago, Christianity is not a natural religion. It has nothing natural in it. It is supernatural from the top to the bottom, from the center, to the circumference, within and without. It comes right from heaven, every bit of it. It is the divine outflow of the Holy Soul of the crucified, risen, glorified Son of God.

Why does God come down from heaven into the hearts of men; into the natures of men; into the bodies of men; into the souls of men; into the spirits of men? God's purpose in man is to transform him into the nature of God. Jesus said, "I said ye are gods." (John 10:34)

The philosophers came to the grave and died. They had no further revelation to give. They had left their nets and they exist to this day. I have studied the great Eastern philosophies. I have searched them from cover to cover. I have read them for years as diligently as I have read my Bible. I have read them to see what their consciousness was. The secret of salvation is not in them.

But in my Bible is seen that the Son of God saves men from their sins, and changes them by His power in their nature, so that they become like Him. And that is the purpose of Jesus, to take a man and make a Christ out of him. To take a sinner and wash him pure and white and clean, and then come into his life and anoint him with His Spirit, speak through him, live in him, change the substance of his spirit, change the substance of his body, until his body and his blood and his bones and flesh and his soul and his spirit, are the body, and blood, and bones, and soul, and spirit of the Son of God (Ephesians 5:30, 1 Corinthians 6:17).

Oh, Jesus was crucified. Jesus was crucified after

there grew in the soul of Jesus the divine consciousness that He could go into the grave, and through faith in God, accept the word of God, and believe that He would raise Him from the dead. Jesus went into the grave with a divine boldness, not simply as a martyr. He was God's Prince, God's King, God's Savior. He went into the grave God's conqueror! He was after something. He went after the power of death, and He got it, and He took it captive, and He came forth from the grave proclaiming His victory over death.

No more bowing before the accursed power that had been generated through sin. It was a captive. No more fear of hell! Do you hear it? No more fear of hell after Jesus Christ came out of the grave. He had death and hell by the throat, and the key in His hands. He was Conqueror!

When He came forth from the grave, He came forth bringing that wonderful spirit of heavenly triumph that was begotten in the soul of Jesus because He had not failed. He had gone and done it. No longer a hope, no longer a faith, now a knowledge of God's consciousness in His heart. It was done!

Oh, yes, bless God, I am coming back to that word which I started. Do you know the secret of religion is in its consciousness? The secret of Christianity is in the consciousness it produces in your soul. And Christianity produces a higher consciousness than any other religion in the world; no other religion in the world, or other revelation of the true God equals it. It is the highest and holiest. It comes breathing and throbbing and burning right out of the heart of the glorified Son of God. It comes breathing and beating and burning and throbbing into your nature and mine, bless God.

So that is the reason I love the religion of the Lord and Savior Jesus Christ. That is the reason the cross of Calvary is a sacred place. That is the reason that the conquest of the Son of God in the world's religions. Death makes a man's heart throb. That is the reason He gathered His disciples together, and as if He could not wait, He said, "Let me breathe it into you. Go forth in its power. All power is given unto me, both in heaven and in earth. Go ye therefore. These signs shall follow…Cast out devils, speak with new tongues…heal the sick." Amen.

In those early centuries of Christianity, Christianity did not go into the world apologizing. It went to slay the powers of darkness and undo the works of the devil, and it lived in holy triumph!

12

CHRIST LIVETH IN ME

That is the text, "Christ liveth in me." That is the revelation of this Age. That is the discovery of the moment. That is the revolutionizing power of God in the earth. It is the factor that is changing the spirit of religion in the world and the character of Christian faith. It is divine vitalization.

The world is awakening to that marvelous truth, that Christ is not in the heavens only, nor in the atmosphere only, but Christ is IN YOU.

The world lived in darkness for thousands of years. There was just as much electricity in the world then as now. It is not that electricity has just come into being. It was always here. But men have discovered how to utilize it and bless themselves with it.

Christ's indwelling in the human heart is the mystery of mysteries. Paul gave it to the Gentiles as the supreme mystery of all the revelation of God and the finality of all wonder he knew. "Christ in you." "Christ in YOU."

Christ has a purpose in you. Christ's purpose in YOU is to reveal Himself to you, through you, in you. We repeat over and over that familiar phrase, "The Church which is His body," but if we realized the truth of it and the power of it, this world would be a different place. When the Christian Church realizes that they are the tangible, living, pulsating body, flesh and bones and blood and brain of Jesus Christ, and that God is manifesting through each one every minute, and is endeavoring to accomplish His big will for the world through them, not through some other body, then Christian service and responsibility will be understood. Jesus Christ operates through you. He does not operate independently of you, He operates through you. Man and God become united. That is the divine secret of a real Christian life. It is the real union, the real conscious union of man and God. There is no substitute for that relationship. You can manufacture all the ordinances on earth, all the symbols there ever were until you become dazed and you lose yourself in the maze of them, and still you must find God.

There is only one reality. That reality is God. The soul of man must contact God, and unless the spirit of man is truly joined to God there is no such thing as real Christian manifestation. All the processes of preparation, by which a soul is prepared by God for such a manifestation, are only preliminary processes. The final end is that man may reveal God and that God may not only have a place of residence but a right action in the body and spirit of man. Every Spirit-taught man in the world is aware of how gradually his own nature has become subjected to God and His will.

I was visiting with a gentleman who had a grouch on me. He said, "I wrote you a twenty-four page letter, and you have not received it. If you had you would not be here." I laughed. That man has been a Christian for thirty or forty years. Always a devout man, and I have spoken of him frequently to my wife and my friends as one of the most consistent Christian men I ever knew. Yet every once in a while we see how the big human just rises up above the spirit and spoils the beauty and delight and wonder of the life that is revealing God.

God's effort and God's purpose in us is to bring all the conditions of our being into harmony with His will and His mind. God's purpose is not to make an automaton. We see a ventriloquist operating a little wooden dummy, and the wooden dummy's lips move and it looks as though it was talking. It is just moving because another power is moving it.

Now God has a higher purpose than making man an automaton. God's highest is to bring out all the qualities of God in your own soul, to bring out all the individuality that is in your life, not to submerge or destroy, but to change it, to energize it, to enlarge it, until all your individuality and personality and being are of the nature and substance and quality of God.

You notice among the most devout Christians how continuously their thought is limited to that place where they can be exercised or moved by God. But God's best is more than that. Receive the Spirit, then use the Spirit for God's glory.

While I was in Chicago I met a couple of old friends who invited me to dinner. While at dinner the lady, who is a very frank woman, said, "Mr. Lake, I have known you so long and have had such close fellowship for so many years, I am able to speak very frankly." I said, "Yes, absolutely." "Well," she said, "there is something I miss about you. For lack of words I am going to put it in Paul's words: 'I bear in my body the marks of the Lord Jesus.' You do not seem to have the marks of Jesus." I said, "That depends whether or not it is the marks of mannerisms. If you are expecting that the personality that God gave me is going to be changed so that I am going to be another fellow and not myself, then you will miss it. If that is the kind of marks you are looking for you will not find them. But if you are expecting to observe a man's flesh and blood and bones and spirit and mind indwelt by God, then you will find them, not a machine, not an automaton, or an imitation, but a clear mind and a pure heart, a son of God in nature and essence."

What is all God's effort with the world but to bring out the real man in the image of Christ, that real man with the knowledge of God, that real man reconstructed until his very substance is the substance of God. And when you stop to reason that to its proper conclusion, that is the only way that Jesus Christ Himself or God the eternal Father will have fellowship with man forever.

When one stops to analyze that fact, we see that

God is trying to make us in all our nature and being and habits and thought, in all the structure of our life, just as beautiful and just as real and just as clear-minded and just as strong as Jesus Himself. Then we understand what Christ's redemption means. It is the bringing out of Christ IN YOU, until Christ in you is the One manifest: manifest through your eyes just as God was manifest through the eyes of Jesus, manifest through your touch just as God was manifest through Jesus. It is not a power nor a life separate from yourself but two lives made one, two natures co-joined, two minds operating as one: Christ in YOU.

In the Chicago conference I sat with an old colored lady one afternoon after the meeting, and she told me of her woes and sicknesses, and they were many. After a time when she had grown somewhat still, I said, "Dear Mother, how long have you been a Christian?" She replied, "Since I was a child." Then I tried to show her that God expected a development of God and His nature and the working and action of God in her in transforming power through the agency of the Holy Spirit, and that there was a process of remaking and remolding that should change her nature and life, and dissolve the rheumatism and Bright's disease and all the other difficulties, just as truly as long ago sin dissolved out of her soul.

After the conversation had gone on to the proper point, I said, "Dear Sister, anybody can see that Christ dwells in your spirit." Her eyes were lovely, delightful. "Let your mind extend just a little bit. Let your thought comprehend that just as Jesus dwells in your spirit and also possesses your soul, in just exactly the same way He is possessing your blood and your kidneys and your old rheumatic bones, and that the very same thing will happen in your bones when you realize that truth as happened in your spirit when you were converted at the altar." (She told me how she had prayed twenty-two days and nights until Christ was revealed in her soul as Savior. She seemed to want to wait twenty-two days and nights for God to manifest Himself in the rheumatic bones, and I was trying to get her away from it.) She said, "Brother, lay your hands on me and pray for me, and I will be healed." I answered, "No, I want you to get well by realizing that right now that same Christ that dwells in your spirit and your soul is in your bones and in your blood and in your brain." Presently the old lady hopped to her feet and said, "My God, He is." She had it. Christ had been imprisoned in her soul and spirit, now He was permitted to manifest in her body.

Brother Tom Hezmalhalch came into a Negro meeting in Los Angeles one day where they were talking about the Baptism of the Holy Ghost. He had picked up a paper and read of these peculiar meetings, and among other things that they spoke in tongues. That was new to him. He said, "If they do, and if it is real, that is an advance in the Spirit of God beyond what is common. I am going to get it." He went, and listened as the old black boy taught. He was trying to develop the thought of conscious cleansing, and he used a beautiful text: "Now ye are clean through the Word which I have spoken unto you." That became very real to Tom, and after a while they were invited to come and kneel at the altar to seek God for the baptism of the Spirit. Tom said unto me, "John, I got up and walked toward that old bench with the realization in my soul of the truth of the Word, and that the real cleansing and cleanser was in my heart. 'Now are ye clean through the Word which I have spoken unto you.'"

He knelt down and he prayed for a minute or two, his soul arose and his heart believed for the baptism of the Holy Ghost. Then he arose and took one of the front seats. One of the workers said, "Brother, don't stop praying until you are baptized in the Holy Ghost." Mr. Seymour said, "Just leave him alone. He has got it. You wait and see." A few days passed, and one day Tom said the Spirit began to surge through him, and a song of praise in tongues, angelic voice, broke through his lips.

An old preacher came into my office in Africa and said, "Brother Lake, there is something I want to talk to you about. There used to be a very remarkable manifestation in my life. It was the manifestation of tongues and interpretation. But I have not spoken for a year. I wish you would pray for me." I said, "No, go over and lie down, and get still and let God move in your life." I went on writing a letter. Presently I observed that something wanted to speak in me, and I turned my head just a little to see that the old man was speaking in tongues and I was getting the interpretation of it as I wrote the letter.

Don't you know Christians are stumbling every day over that fact. You are doubting and fearing and wondering if Christ is there. Beloved brother and sister, give Him a chance to reveal Himself. He is there. Probably because of your lack of realization your soul is closed and He is not able to reveal Himself. You know God is never able in many to reveal Himself outside of the spirit or soul. The real secret of the ministry of healing is in permitting the grace of God in your heart to flow out through your hands and your nerves into the outer life. That is the real secret, and one of the greatest works God has to perform is to subject our flesh to God. Many Christians, the deepest Christians who really know God in their spirits and enjoy communion with God, are compelled to wait until there is a process of spiritualization takes place in their bodies before God can reveal Himself through them. Do not imprison Christ in you. Let Him live, let Him manifest, let Him vent through you.

There is one great thing that the world is needing more than anything else, and I am convinced of it every day I live. Mankind has one supreme need, and that is the LOVE of God. The hearts of men are dying for lack of the love of God. I have a sister in Detroit. She came over to Milwaukee to visit us for two or three days at the convention there. As I watched her moving around, I said, "I would like to take her along and just have her love folks." She would not need to preach. You do not need to preach to folks. It is not the words you say that are going to bless them. They need something greater. It is the thing in your soul. They have got to receive it, then their soul will open and there will be a divine response. Give it to them: it is the love of God.

You have seen people who loved someone who would not respond. If there is any hard situation in God's earth, that is it, to really passionately love someone and find no response in them.

I had an English friend and was present at his marriage. Some years later he and his wife came to visit our home. He was the cold type of closed up Englishman, and his wife was the warm type. One day as they started out for a walk, I noticed the passionate yearning in her soul. If he would just say something that was tender, something that would gratify the craving of her nature for affection, but he seemed to go along absolutely unconscious of it. After a while they came back from their walk. I was sitting on the front steps. After the lady had gone into the house, I said, "Hibbs, you are a stiff. How is it possible that you can walk down the street with a woman like your wife and not realize that her heart is craving and crying for you to turn around and do something that shows you love her?" He said, "Do you think that is the difficulty? I will go and do it now." And everything subsided while he proceeded to do it.

What is it men are seeking? What is it their hearts

are asking for when they are seeking God? What is their soul crying for? Mankind is separated from God. It may not be mountains of sin between you and God at all. It may be that your nature is closed and unresponsive. My! When the real love touch of God is breathed into your soul, what a transformation takes place. There is probably no more delightful thing on earth than to watch a soul praying into God, when the light of God comes in and the life of God fills the nature and that holy affection that we seek from others finds expression in Him.

That is what the Lord is asking from you, and if you want to gratify the heart of Jesus Christ, that is the only way in all the world to do it. You know the invitation is not "Give Me thine head." The invitation is, "My son, give Me thine HEART." That is an affectionate relationship, a real love union in God, a real love union with God. Think of the fineness of God's purpose. He expects that same marvelous spiritual union that is brought to pass between your soul and His own to be extended so that you embrace in that union every other soul around you.

Oh, that is what it means when it talks about being baptized in one spirit, submerged, buried, enveloped and enveloping in the one Spirit of God.

While I was in Milwaukee recently, I went out one morning with Rev. Fockler to make a call on a sick person. We stepped into one of the most distracted homes I have ever been in. A strange condition had developed in one of the daughters, and the household was distressed. They were the saddest group. They were German people. Fockler speaks German. Presently he began to talk to the household. I just sat back and watched. Presently I noticed the faces began to relax and the strain was gone. The girl was apparently insane. She came down the stairs, stood outside the door where she could not be seen except by me. He continued to converse with the family, and as their souls softened and their faith lifted, her eyes commenced to change. She was moved upon by the same Spirit until her nature responded, and in just a little while she stepped into the room. She had tormented that household. Nobody could get near her. She slipped up behind Fockler's chair, stood with her hands on the back of the chair. He understood and disregarded. After a little while she put the other hand on the other shoulder. And in fifteen or twenty minutes we left that home, and there was just as much distinction between the attitude of those dear people when we came in and when we left as between heaven and hell. If hell has a characteristic, it is that of distraction. If heaven has a particular characteristic, it is the presence of God, the calm of God, the power of God, the love of God.

There were days when the Church could club men into obedience by preaching hell to them, but that day has long passed. The world has outgrown it. And men are discovering there is only one way and that is the Jesus way. Jesus did not come with a club, but with the great loving heart of the Son of God. He was "moved with compassion."

This morning I lay in bed and wrote a letter, an imaginary letter to a certain individual. I was getting ready so that when I came down I could dictate the sentences that would carve him right. One of the phrases was, "You great big calf, come out of it and be a man." As I lay there I got to thinking, "If Jesus was writing this letter, I wonder what He would write?" But somehow it would not frame. My soul was not in an attitude to produce such a letter. So I came down this morning and called Edna and commenced to dictate, and I was trying to dictate a letter in the Spirit of Jesus. Presently I woke up to the fact that I was putting the crimp into it like a lawyer. After she had written it and laid it down for me to sign, I commenced to read it over. It was not what I wanted to write at all. The first two paragraphs had a touch of the right spirit but that was all. So I laid it aside. Then I went in and prayed a little while. After I had been praying for twenty minutes, the telephone rang. It was that fellow. He wanted me to come down to the Davenport Hotel. We had three of the best hours without being aware of the time.

We boast of our development in God; we speak glowingly of our spiritual experiences, but it is only once in a while that we find ourselves in the real love of God. The greater part of the time we are in ourselves rather than in Him. That evidences just one thing, that Christ has not yet secured that perfect control of our life, that subjection of our nature, that absorption of our individuality, so that He is able to impregnate it and maintain it in Himself. We recede, we draw back, we close up. We imprison our Lord.

The secret of a religious meeting is that it assists men's hearts to open. They become receptive, and the love of God finds vent in their nature for a little while, and they go away saying, "Didn't we have a good time? Wasn't that a splendid meeting?"

I wonder if there is anything that could not be accomplished through that love of God. Paul says there is not. "Love never faileth." That is one infallible state. Try it on your wife, try it on your children, try it on your neighbors.

Ah, sometimes we need to get things over on to the bigger love, the greater heart. It is a good thing to detach your soul. Do not hold people. Do not bind people. Just cut them loose and let God love them. Don't you know we hold people with such a grip when we pray for them that they miss the blessing. Why, you have such a grip on your humanity that it is exercising itself and the spirit is being submerged. Let your soul relax and let the Spirit of God in you find vent. There is no substitute for the love of God. "Christ in you." Oh, you have the capacity to love. All the action of the Spirit of God has its secret there.

I stood on one occasion by a dying woman who was suffering and writhing in awful agony. I had prayed again and again with no results. But this day something just happened inside of me. My soul broke clear down, and I saw that poor soul in a new light.

Before I knew it I reached out and gathered her in my arms and hugged her up to my soul, not my bosom. In a minute I knew the real thing had taken place. I laid her back down on the pillow. In five minutes she was well. God was waiting on me until He could get to my soul the sense of that tenderness that was in the Son of God.

That is the reason that His Name is written in imperishable memory. And the Name of Jesus Christ is the most revered Name in earth or sea or sky. And I am eager to get in that category of folks who can manifest the real love of God all the time.

The real Christian is a SEPARATED man. He is separated forever unto God in ALL the departments of his life. So his Body, so his Soul and his Spirit are forever committed to God the Father. From the time he commits himself to God, his BODY is as absolutely in the hands of God as his spirit or his soul. He can go to no other power for help or healing.

An hundredfold consecration takes the individual forever out of the hands of all but God.

"Ye are not your own."

13

REIGN AS KINGS

I want to bring you a message that came to me today. I have been for years on the verge of this message, but never did I receive it until this morning. In the fifth chapter of Romans and the seventeenth verse in another translation there is a remarkable rendering:

"For if by the trespass of the one, death reigned as king through the one, much more shall they who receive the abundance of grace and the gift of righteousness reign as kings in the realm of life, through Jesus Christ" (Romans 5:17).

That means that the moment you accept Jesus Christ, God becomes your righteousness. That is the "gift of righteousness." Let me read it again: "For if by the trespass of the one, death reigned as king through the one, much more shall they who receive the abundance of grace and the gift of righteousness reign as kings in the realm of life through Jesus Christ." It means everyone of us that have been born again come into a kingly and queenly state, and we are accepted by God to reign as kings and queens in the realm of life.

We have reigned as servants in the realm of spiritual death. We have passed out of death, Satan's realm, into the realm of life, into the realm of the supernatural, or the spiritual, or the heavenlies.

Here are some significant facts. Man was never made a slave. He was never made for slavery. He was made to reign as king under God. If you noticed, I showed you this, that the kingly being that was created was created in the image and likeness of God, that he was created on terms of equality with God that he could stand in the presence of God without any consciousness of inferiority.

I quote you from the eighth Psalm in which this expression is used:

"What is man that thou art mindful of Him? And the son of man, that Thou visitest Him? For Thou hast made him but little lower than God; and crownest him with glory and honor" (Psalm 8:4-5).

(In Psalm 8:4-5 the word "angel" is from the Hebrew "Elohim" and is the name of God in the first five chapters of Genesis.)

What does it mean? It means that God has made us as near like Himself as it is possible for God to make a being. He made you in His image. He made you in His likeness. He made you the same class of being that He is Himself.

He made Adam with an intellect, with such calibre that he was able to name every animal, every

144

vegetable, and every fruit, and give them names that would fit and describe their characteristics. When God could do that with man, then that man belonged to the realm of God.

Adam had such vitality in his body that even after he sinned and became mortal he lived nearly a thousand years: 930 years before mortality got in its work and put him on his death bed. Methuselah lived 969 years. Life was so abundant, so tremendous in their minds and spirits that it conquered century after century.

Jesus said: "I am come that ye might have life, and that ye might have it abundantly."

More abundantly! Jesus made the declaration: "I am come that ye might have life."

The thing that was forfeited in the garden was regained. God gave him dominion over the works of His hand. God made him His understudy, His king, to rule over everything that had life. Man was master. Man lived in the realm of God. He lived on terms of equality with God. God was a faith God. All God had to do was to believe that the sun was, and the sun was. All God had to do was to believe that the planets would be, and they were. Man belonged to God's class of being: a faith man. And he lived in the creative realm of God. Friends, if you believe what I am preaching, it is going to end your impotence and weakness and you will swing out into a power such as you have never known in your life.

Man lost his place by high treason against God. He lost his dominion in the fall. With the fall went his dominion over spirit and soul. But universal man over yearned for the return of his dominion.

Brother, do you hear me? Here is one of the most tremendous facts that we have to face, that never a single primitive people that has ever been found that has not yearned for dominion. Not a single primitive people has been found that did not have a Golden Past where they had dominion, a Golden Future where dominion was going to be restored. That is the tradition of universal man.

Man has craved dominion. Man has shrunk from bondage. Man has rebelled against it. Man has yearned to gain the mastery again over physical loss, over mind loss, and over the loss of spirit. This long ago desire to gain the lost dominion is seen in his offerings, in his drinking blood, in his priesthood that he has appointed.

I want to enter this a little bit with you. Darwin foolishly said that the reason man drank blood was because the blood was salty and he craved salt. Friends, human blood was never desirable to any people. Why did they drink it? They drank it in order that they might be like God. They drank it that they might become eternal, immortal.

The desire of immortality of the physical body lies latent in the heart of universal man. And for that reason they drank it, believing if they drank it they would be like God. They took the animal or man, and they laid it upon the altar of their god or gods, and when they did they believed that the offering became identified with their god. Then they said, "If we drink the blood of the man or animal, we drink the blood of God, and if we drink enough of it, we will be God."

How far is that removed from the communion table? Do you see the analogy? The communion table is practically unknown as yet to the majority of Christians.

Now the ancients believed this, and the people of Africa, and it caused them to become cannibals. It was not because they loved human blood, but they believed if they could eat the flesh and drink the blood that was given to their god, they would be like God. You will find that all through the legends and poetry of the old world.

Universal man feels the lost dominion can be regained. They have a conviction that it is going to be regained. And this faith of universal man, reaching Godward, finally challenged God to make it a possibility. He believes that union with God will give him this dominion. He hates defeat. He wants to conquer death. He dreams of immortality. He fears death and disease.

Let me recapitulate. This universal man has believed that somewhere God was going to give him this lost dominion. He believed that that dominion would come through His union with God, if that union could be effected. Can you understand now? It was the universal knowledge and the universal need and the universal cry of man for union with Deity that caused the incarnation.

Let me come a step closer. On the ground of what Jesus Christ did, the substitutionary sacrifice, God is able to redeem us from our sins. He is able to impart to us His very nature. He is able to give us eternal life, take us into His own family, so that we can call Him, "Father." Not by adoption only, but by an actual birth of our spirit, so we come into actual relationship and union with God, and the age old cry of universal man has been fulfilled. Do you see? The new birth has brought us into vital union with Jesus Christ.

This thing I am teaching you about our union with God is not known in the great body of Christians. All they have is forgiveness of sin. There is no actual union with God. They do not know that the new Birth is a real incarnation. They do not know that they are as much the sons and daughters of God Almighty as Jesus is. The great body of the Christian Church has no dominion, does not know it. They have the most befogged concept of what God has done and what God is to them and what they are to God.

Another step. The incarnation that God has given through the new Birth has bestowed upon us the lost authority of the Garden of Eden. And only here and there has a man known it or preached it or dared to assume it.

Let me break in here. J. Hudson Taylor, after his

first visit to China, was walking in England and a voice said, "If you will walk with Me, we will evangelize Inland China." He looked and there was no one there. An unseen angel had spoken to him. Then his heart caught the vision and said, "Lord, we will do it." He was the founder of the Great Inland China Mission.

Taylor was returning on a sailing vessel and they were going through the Yellow Sea. It was in the section where the seven winds come at eventide, but from a certain hour in the day until evening there is no wind. One afternoon the Captain said to Mr. Taylor, "Take this." And he took the glasses and looked. He could see they were nearing land. The Captain said, "The worst pirates in all this awful section of the ocean are there. Our vessel is in the clutches of the tide and in three hours will strike the rocks and there is no hope of saving it." J. Hudson said, "Are you a Christian?" He said, "I am." Taylor asked, "Are there any other Christians here?" He said, "Yes, the cook and the carpenter and another man are Christians." Taylor said, "Call them, and let's go pray." He called them and the five or six of them went to their respective places. They had not been praying but a little while when he heard commands being given on board and men rushing about. He came up, and he could see the wind breaking on the sea that had been so glassy. In a few minutes the wind had filled the sails, three hours before nature would have sent it.

In my own experience I have seen God many

times set aside natural law. I told you one day about one miracle. We were putting on a roof on one of our buildings. A storm came up. The boys had unwisely torn off too many shingles for us to cover before the storm reached us. I saw that storm go around us and leave ten or fifteen acres where the rain did not fall for more than one-half hour, and the water flowed down the gutters past our buildings. Those boys worked and sang and shouted. When the last shingle was in place the water fell on it, and we were drenched to the skin. I have seen God perform His prodigies in answer to believing prayer. What God does for one He can do for another.

This inferiority complex that makes men seek God and create religions and priesthoods is a relic of the fall and comes because man is conscious that once somewhere he had power, he had dominion, and he galls under it. Like a mighty athlete that feels his strength leaving him, until by and by he becomes helpless as a little child. Oh, the agony of the thing!

Every man has within him the entire history of every man. That cry of agony of the athlete, that cry of agony of the man that once had physical and mental health is the cry of universal man, crying for the lost authority and dominion that he once enjoyed. He seeks through rites a new birth, a re-creation that does not come. How many lodges and secret societies have a rite, a symbol of the New Birth. I can not mention them, but you look back. You are initiated into such and such an organization. I can name four that have a New Birth rite. It is latent in the universal man.

Every religion has some kind of re-creation. Why? Every man has a consciousness (I am speaking of men who think) down in them. There is something that cries out against death, against sickness, against sorrow, against defeat, against failure. There is something that revels against the bondage of fear and that cries for rebirth, a re-creation that will give them dominion and mastery over the forces that have held them in bondage.

Our redemption is God's answer to this universal hunger. We saw God's hunger creating man; now you see man's hunger bringing God to recreate him. Can't you understand it, men, that the hunger in the heart of God drove Him, forced Him, until He spoke a world into being for the home of His love project, man. It has driven Him to create universes to hold this world by the law of attraction and make it a safe place for man.

Then when man fell and lost his standing and became a slave and subject to Satan, then this universal cry went up until the very heart of God bled for this broken human. Then He made provision whereby this man that He had created, and had sinned and had de-created, might come back into fellowship with Him of a higher, holier sort than he had lost at the beginning.

I want to take you through some scriptures. Go with me to Romans 5:17;

"For if by the trespass of one, death reigned as king, through the one, much more shall they who receive the abundance of grace and the gift of righteousness, reign as kings in the realm of life through Jesus Christ."

By the New Birth you have passed out of Satan's dominion and Satan's power and you have come over into God's dominion, and you have come over into the kingdom of the Son of His love.

You will pardon me, but I have this consciousness when I am preaching: there comes up a wave from the congregation of a kind of stultified unbelief. Do you know where it comes from? It comes from all the years you have sat under false teachers. You have been taught that to be humble you have got to say you are a sinner, you are no good, you don't amount to anything. You sing:

"Weak and sickly, vile and full of sin I am."

I do not like to preach one thing, and Charles Wesley another. If you are born again, you are a son of God. And for you to tear yourself out of your sonship, your relationship and the righteousness of God, and put yourself over in the realm of death, and tell God you are dirty and unclean, that His blood has not cleansed you, and His life has not been delivered you, it is a monstrous thing. It is all right to sing that as an unregenerate, but it is not the experience of the sons and daughters of God.

Here is our position through Jesus Christ. God has become our righteousness. We have become His very sons and daughters, and you sing weakness, and you talk weakness and you pray weakness, and you sing unbelief, and you pray and talk it, and you go out and live it. You are like that good old woman. She said: "I do love that doctrine of falling from grace, and I practice it all the time." Another man said, "Brother, I believe in the dual nature. I believe that when I would do good, evil is always present with me, and I thank God that evil is always there." You live it and believe it, and God can not do anything with you. You magnify failure and you deify failure until to the majority of you the devil is bigger than God. And you are more afraid of the devil than you are of God. You have more reverence for the devil than you do for God. It is absolutely true. If any saint would dare to say, "I am done with disease and sickness; I will never be sick again," ninety percent of you would say, "Keep your eyes on that person. He will be sick in a week. The devil sure will get him." You believe the devil is bigger than God. Your God is about one and a half inches high and the devil is one and a half feet high. What you need to do is to change gods and change gods quick. There have been only a few folks that had a good-sized God.

You go over in Genesis and you see the size of God. It is a full-sized photograph. You see Jesus Christ rising from the dead, and you have seen the

God-sized photograph of redemption. We "reign as kings in the realm of life." And what is the reaction in you? You say, "That is all right and I wish that was true in my case. I would like to reign as king." And you think this moment how you are whipped, and you think how you have been defeated, and how weak you are, and you will be defeated all the next week. You reckon on the strength of the devil, and on your own sickness, You say, "If he had what I have he wouldn't talk like that." How can the potter of God come through such a mess of unbelief? How can God get near? Ninety percent of those who have received the Spirit have made God a little bit of a side issue, a sort of court of last resort. When you get where the devil can do no more, you say, "God, catch me. The devil has finished his work." God is simply a Life Insurance Company that pays the premium at death.

Turn with me to Ephesians 1:7;

"In whom we have redemption through his blood, the forgiveness of our trespasses, according to the riches of his grace."

For months and months that scripture has been burning its way into my soul. "In whom we have our redemption through his blood, the forgiveness of our trespasses," and it is "according to the riches of his grace." It is illustrated in Israel coming out of Egypt, with the Red Sea before them, with vast desert stretching its burning waste between them and their

154

promised land. We do not have any such redemption in our religion. I'll tell you what we need. Have you been in Canada? Do you know when we went to Canada for the first time there was one thing that struck me peculiarly. The signs would read, "John Brown, Limited." Everywhere I saw that sign. That is a Scotchmen's caution. I was holding meetings in the old St. Andrews Church in Sidney. I asked them one night why they did not put their national symbol on their Churches. They wondered what I meant. I said, "Every other business house is 'LTD.' Why don't you put it over the Church?" An old Scotchman said, "We don't have to. Everybody knows it." Limited? Sure it is limited. Limit God, limit ourselves, limit His grace, limit the Word. Sure, our God is a little bit of a god. Most of us could carry Him in our vest pocket, and it wouldn't bulge the pocket. Our God with the "LTD" on him.

Brother, sister, that challenge comes to us today to let God loose. There are a few places where they have let God have His way, and how the blessings have come.

"In whom we have our redemption."

Have you? If you have your redemption it means that to you Satan has been defeated. Jesus conquered the devil as a Jew before He died. Then He let the devil conquer Him on the cross and send Him down to the place of suffering with our burden and guilt upon Him. But after He satisfied the claims of justice Jesus met the devil in his own throne room and He stripped him of his authority and dominion. And when He arose He said:

"I am He that liveth, and was dead: and, behold, I am alive for evermore, and have the keys of hell and of death" (Revelation 1:18).

He had gone into the throne room, taken Satan's badge of dominion and authority that Adam had given him in the Garden of Eden. And every man that accepts Jesus Christ was identified with Him when He did it. He did it for you. He did it for me. He died as our substitute and representative. When He put his heel on Satan's neck, He did it for you, and you were in Christ. And to you who believe, Satan is conquered and Satan is defeated. Satan can holler and bellow as much as he wants to, but you withstand him in the faith of Jesus Christ.

I saw a picture this morning. I was reading an article. I saw a company of men walk out, and I saw all the diseases and all the crimes and agonies; I saw cancers and tumors and tuberculosis; and I saw a company of men and women walk down in the midst of it, and I heard them say, "Here come the sons of God: here come the conquerors." And the sons of God said to disease, "In the name of Jesus, depart," and disease fled. It fled as it did before the Son of God. It obeyed because the Son of God sent them out and gave them His name as authority. I saw the company of men enter into the lost dominion. They put upon them the garments of their authority and dominion and walked out conquerors over death and hell and the grave. They were masters. They were rulers.

Then I saw another picture. I saw David in the old cave of Adullam. I saw men coming down that were broken and in distress and in debt, and men that were in awful physical conditions. And they gathered four hundred strong around David. And out of that crowd David developed and trained the most invincible army that was ever seen. Then my mind passed over a few years of struggle. And I saw from that company some mighty men come forth. I saw one man come forth and go where there were thousands and thousands of Philistines; men that were shoulders above him; men that wore shields. I saw that man go among those giants and he slew hundreds of them. And I piled them up in hundreds until I had piled eight hundred.

Every one of those mighty men of David were simple men of extraordinary ability. There was no mark to indicate that they were more than common Jews, 5' 11", but they knocked down men 6' 6" and 6' 8". They conquered them because they were blood covenant men.

That is the type of the Church of Jesus Christ. And I said, "Where are God's mighty men today?" Then I saw a picture. David sat there a little way from the spring of Bethlehem, and the Philistines had got control of the water. David said, "Oh, that I had a drink." And those three men came forth. He said, "Where are you going, boys?" They just waved him off, and those three men conquered the whole company of the Philistines, filled their pitchers with water, and set them down at David's feet.

I cried, "My God, my God, where are the mighty men of valor of today, the men that can assail the forces of Satan?" God says they are coming out of you; they are going to arrive. God has in training some men and women that are going to do exploits for Him. Will you not come up and live in your realm?

This is the trouble with most of us. We live up in the faith realm, but we have gone down the back stairs into the reason realm, and a lot of you are hugging your old devilish reason right now.

God help you, brother, this afternoon to throw your reason out that has led you into all kinds of doubt and fear, to throw it to the wind and say, "God, here goes. We trust in your omnipotence to put it over."

14

LAKE'S REPLY TO DR. ELWOOD BULGIN

(This letter was printed in the leading daily newspaper in Spokane, Washington, 1920)

Spokane, Washington
February 28, 1920

Dr Elwood Bulgin,
Spokane, Washington

Dear Brother in Christ:

It was my privilege to be present at your meeting at the St. Paul Methodist Church at Spokane last Monday night and listen to your sermon. I was deeply impressed by the masterful manner in which you marshaled your facts, and the spirit in which they were presented to your great audience.

Your presentation of the deity of Jesus Christ, and the sharpness with which you brought the facts of the denial of the deity of Jesus by the Christian Scientists, were striking. The masterful handling of the whole subject commanded my admiration, and I believe the admiration of a great majority of your audience.

Men can speak with frankness to each other,

particularly when their interest in the Kingdom of Jesus Christ are identical. You have lived, loved, and denied yourself, and suffered for the cause of the Kingdom of Christ in the earth. I, too, have loved and suffered for my fidelity to the vision of the redemption of Jesus Christ which God revealed to me.

For twenty-five years I have labored, as few men in the world have labored for so long a period, to bring before the world as far as I could the magnificent truths of the redemptive blood and life and power of the Son of God.

Your methods and my methods have been different. You, in your forceful, philosophical manner, have undertaken to destroy faith in Christian Science through opposition, ridicule, and exposure of what you believe to be its fallacies. On the other hand I have undertaken by specific revelation of the truth of Jesus Christ concerning the healing power of God and its availability for all men today to show the world that there is no need for any man to leave any stable Christian body in order to secure the benefits of salvation and healing specifically declared by Jesus Christ Himself to be available for every man.

Jesus, in contrast with the ancient philosophers and reformers of the past and present, first gave Himself in consecration to God, body, soul and spirit, thereby establishing the pattern consecration for all Christians forever. His baptism was the dedication and commitment of Himself "unto all righteousness." He undertook to reveal the righteousness of God. Note the nature of this revelation.

Having definitely committed Himself, His body, His soul, His spirit, to God forever, immediately there descended upon Him the witness to His hundredfold consecration. The Holy Ghost came from heaven as a dove and abode upon Him, as it ever will upon every man who will meet Almighty God with the same utterances of real consecration to God, of spirit and soul and body. This reveals the demand of God upon the Christians' person and conscience, and the answer of God from heaven to this fullness of consecration.

Being thus definitely equipped, He proceeded to the wilderness for testing by Satan to see if this consecration of body and soul and spirit would endure.

He overcame all the efforts of Satan to tempt him in the specific departments of His life; first, the body; second, the soul; third, the spirit. He overcame through reliance on God and His word, and came forth in the power of the Spirit. He announced the constructive platform of His life and ministry, containing the following six planks:

"The Spirit of the Lord is upon me, because He hath anointed me."

First—"To preach the gospel to the poor."
Second—"He hath sent me to heal the broken hearted."

Third—"To preach deliverance to the captives."

Fourth—"Recovering of sight to the blind."

Fifth—"To set at liberty them that are bruised."

Sixth—"To preach the acceptable year of the Lord."

God's acceptable year had come. No more waiting for the year of Jubilee and all its consequent blessings. God's never-ending Jubilee was at hand in Jesus Christ.

He then went throughout all Galilee teaching in their synagogues, and preaching the gospel of the Kingdom, and healing all manner of sickness and all manner of disease among the people, and so established forever the ideal of Christian ministry for the Church of God.

Then He empowered twelve men, and "sent them to preach the Kingdom of God, and to heal the sick." Profiting by their experience, and advancing in faith and knowledge of the power of God, He "called seventy others also." But in sending forth the seventy He reversed the order of instruction. To the seventy He said, "Go into the cities round about. Heal the sick that are therein, and say to them, the Kingdom of God is come nigh unto you." And they returned rejoicing that even the devils were subject to them "through thy name."

Then came His Wonderful entrance into death, His redemption on the cross, His resurrection from the grave, His interviews with His disciples, His last commission in which, according to Mark, He established in the Church of Christ, to be born through their preaching in all the world, the very same ministry of salvation and healing that He himself during His earth life had practiced. That ministry contained the message of Jesus to all the world and the anointing with power from on High, just as He had received it at His baptism. Indeed He commanded them to wait in Jerusalem until "Ye shall be baptized with the Holy Ghost, not many days hence."

He declared to them that certain signs should follow, saying, "These signs shall follow them that believe." Every one, every Christian soul, was thus commissioned by Jesus to heal the sick and sinful from sickness and sin.

"In my name shall they:"

First—"Cast out devils."

Second—"They shall speak with new tongues."

Third—"They shall take up serpents."

Fourth—"And if they drink any deadly thing, it shall not hurt them."

Fifth—"They shall lay hands on the sick and they shall recover."

The same Holy Spirit of God which flowed through Jesus Christ, the anointing that was upon Him and which flowed through His hands and into the sick, was an impartation of God so real that when the woman touched the hem of His garment she was conscious of the instant effect of the healing in her body through it. "She felt in her body that she was healed of that plague," while Jesus Himself was likewise conscious of an outflow. He said: "Somebody hath touched me, for I perceive that virtue is gone out of me."

Divine Healing is the particular phase of ministry in which the modern Church does not measure up to the Early Church. This failure has been due to a lack of knowledge of the real nature and the real process of Christian Healing. The above incident reveals the secret of what the power was, how the power operated, by what law it was transmitted from the disciple to the one who needed the blessing. The power was the Holy Ghost of God, both in Jesus Christ after His baptism in the Holy Ghost, and in the disciples after the baptism of the Holy Ghost came upon them on the day of Pentecost. It flowed through the hands of Jesus to the sick, it permeated the garments He wore. When the woman touched even the hem of His garment there was sufficient of the power of God there for her need.

The disciples healed the sick by the same method. Indeed, the apostle Paul, realizing this law, permitted the people to bring to him handkerchiefs and aprons that they might touch his body, and when they were carried to the sick, the sick were healed through the power of God in the handkerchiefs, and the demons that inhabited their persons went out of them.

Herein is shown the secret of the early Church, that which explains the whole miracle-working power of the apostles and the early Church for four hundred years. The same is evident in branches of the modern Church. Herein is revealed the secret that has been lost. That secret is the conscious, tangible, living, incoming, abiding, outflowing Spirit of God through the disciple of Christ who has entered into blood-washed relationship and baptism in the Holy Ghost.

This is the secret that the modern Church from the days of the Reformation onward has failed to reveal. We have, however, retained a form of godliness, "but have denied the power thereof."

When Jesus laid His hands on people, the Holy Ghost was imparted to them in healing virtue. When the disciples and early Christians likewise laid their hands on the sick, the Holy Ghost was imparted through them to the needy one. Likewise the Holy Ghost was imparted to preachers "for the work of the ministry," including healing. Primitive Church history abounds in examples of healing in the same manner. Paul specifically enjoins Timothy to "forget not the gift (power) that is in thee, that came through the laying on of my hands." It was an impartation of the Holy Ghost to Timothy for the work of the Christian ministry.

In the whole range of Church history we have retained the form, but have lost its power in a great degree. The pope lays his hands on the head of the Cardinals, the Cardinal lays his hands on the head of

165

the Bishops, the Bishop lays his hands on the head of the Priest, the Priest lays his hands on the head of the communicants when he receives them as members of the Church.

In the Protestant Church in all her branches, the laying on of hands in ordination for the ministry is practiced. But in the early Church it was not the laying on of hands alone, but through the laying on of hands the impartation of the definite living Spirit of the living God to the individual took place. Through its power in him he was constituted a real priest, a real elder, a real preacher with grace, healing power and faith anointed of God from on High.

God gave the blood of Jesus to the Christian Church. God gave the power of healing to the Christian Church in the Holy Ghost, and as long as they lived under the anointing of the Holy Ghost and exercised the faith of Jesus in their hearts, the healing power of God manifested and is still manifest where this condition exists. Christian Science exists because of the failure of the Christian Church to truly present Jesus Christ and His power through the Spirit and minister it to the world.

Robert G. Ingersoll assailed the Holy Scriptures, laughed at the Christian God, destroyed the faith of men, wrecked their hopes and left them stranded and abandoned amid the wreckage. Through this means he brought the just condemnation of the world upon himself. The world condemns him to this hour in that he destroyed the faith of men without supplying to their souls something to take its place, as he should have done, and as any man who is honorable and true must do.

You recommended Divine Healing in one breath and denied its potency in the next. You have attacked Christian Science, the followers of Dowie, and others and arraigned them at the bar and condemned them, without giving to men a tangible way by which the healing of God might be brought to them. Why do you not study and practice Jesus Christ's own way of healing and so make your ministry constructive? What are you going to do with the multitude of dying that the doctors can not help? Leave them to die? The doctors have got through with them. And in many instances even though they are still prescribing for them and are perfectly aware of their inability to heal the sick ones and are candid and willing to say so. Dr Bulgin, what have you got for these? What have you given to these?

If a man were walking down the street with a very poor set of crutches and a ruffian came along and kicked the crutches from under him and let him fall, every honest soul would rise in condemnation of the ruffian's act and demand reparation.

You come to the dying, kick their hope from under them, and let them fall to the ground, and leave them there to die without bringing them the true healing power in the blood and Spirit of Jesus. It is not sufficient to say "I believe in Divine healing." If they are sick they must be healed.

This must not be construed as a defense of Christian Science. It is not given with that thought, nor in that spirit. It is given rather in the hope that as an influential man in the Christian Church, you may see the weakness of your position and of the position of the Church, and by the grace of God call the Church back again to faith in Jesus Christ, the Son of God, for healing for every man from every disease, as Jesus Christ intended it should be and as the scriptures definitely, positively teach, and make proper scriptural provision for a definite healing ministry.

In the hope of supplying this need of the Church, the Protestant ministers of the city of Los Angeles have agreed in formal resolution to begin the teaching and study and practice of healing. How has this come to pass, and why? They have been whipped into it by the success of Christian Science.

A recent issue of a New York daily paper announces that the pastors of New York have likewise undertaken to teach the people the power of God to heal.

The Protestant Episcopal Church is endeavoring through the ministry of a layman of the Church of England from the old country, a Mr. Hickson, to educate their people in the truth of healing through the atonement of Jesus Christ, the Son of God, by the laying on of hands and the prayer of faith. In a few days the gentleman will appear at All Saints Cathedral, Spokane, for that purpose, and the sick will be invited to be ministered to in the name of the Son of God and healed through His blood purchase. The Church of England in England and also in Africa for ten years has been endeavoring to organize societies, not to teach their people Christian Science, psychic therapeutics, or mental healing, all of which belong to the realm of the natural, but to teach and demonstrate the pure power of God from Heaven by the Holy Ghost, purchased by the blood of Jesus Christ, to heal diseases.

Frank N. Riale, a secretary of the Presbyterian Board of Education of New York, with sixty-three universities and colleges under his control and supervision, is the author of a remarkable book, "The Sinless, Sickless, Deathless Life," in which he recounts in a chapter entitled "How the Light and the Fire Fell" the marvelous story of his own conversion. He was a minister of the Gospel and a graduate of Harvard. He found his Lord at the hands of an Indian in Dakota. He tells of the light of God that came to his soul in sanctifying power through the ministry of a Salvation Army officer, Colonel Brengle. He related his marvelous healing, when a diseased and dying wreck, through the reading of a religious tract on healing and his experience in seeing many healed of all manner of diseases by the power of God. You are a Presbyterian, my Brother. You need not go out of your own Church for the truth of God concerning healing.

The question before the Church, now that the break toward healing has come, and it has come, is who is prepared to teach and demonstrate the truth of God concerning healing? Will it be a fact that in the absence of knowledge of God by the ministry of the Church for healing, will the Church in her blindness and ignorance and helplessness be overwhelmed by Christian Science, New Thought and the thousand and one cults which teach psychological healing?

There is the prophet of God who should come forward, teach and demonstrate the pure spiritual value and power of the Holy Ghost, secured for men because Jesus Christ, the Son of God, gave His blood to get it for them? Is it not time that such men as yourself arise in the dignity of Christ and throw off the shackles of formal religion and by the grace of God enter into the real life of living power through the Son of God in the Holy Ghost, and rescue the Church out of her present degradation, re-establishing forever Divine Healing on its true and scriptural basis, the atonement of Jesus Christ?

Twenty-five years ago the light concerning healing came to my soul, after four brothers and four sisters had died of diseases, and when four other members of the family were in a dying state, abandoned by the physicians as hopeless, and after my father had spent a fortune trying to obtain human help. One man of God who had the truth of God in his heart came to the rescue. All four sick ones were healed. I was an ardent Methodist. I loved my Church. My parents were members of an old Scotch Presbyterian Kirk,

The Presbyterian Church had no light on the subject of healing; the Methodist Church had no light on the subject of healing. I received my light through a man who had been a minister of the Congregational Church. He knew God. He knew Christ the Lord. He knew the power of God to save, and the power of God to heal.

When I accepted this blessed truth and saw my family healed out of death, what was the attitude of the Church? Just what the attitude of all the leading Churches has been. When I declared this truth before our conferences, she undertook to ostracize me; and from that day to this many, of her ministry, who have prayed through to God and secured the blessing and power of God upon their soul to heal the sick, have been forced out of her ministry.

Dr Bulgin, is it not time to quit attacking forms of faith, whether good or bad, and turn your attention and the attention of the Church to the only thing that will deliver her out of her present wretchedness and inability to bless, and to bring her back again to Christ, to the foot of the cross, to the blood of Jesus, to the Holy Ghost from on High, to the power of God and the real faith including healing, "once delivered to the saints." Through this healing ministry the Church at Spokane reports 100,000 healings by the power of God through five years of continuous daily efforts and the kindred blessed fact that the majority of those healed were saved from sin also. The dying world is stretching out her hands for help.

The Church on account of her laxness in this matter opens the doors for the existence of Christian Science and all the thousand and one worn out philosophies that follow in her train. Let the manhood of the Church arise, take the place of the prophet of God, call her back to the ministry of real salvation, a blessed salvation not alone for men after they are dead, or that will give them bliss in heaven when they die, but to a salvation that gives eternal life in Christ, health for the mind, and health for the body, and supplies likewise the power of God for the immediate need, for the need of the sick, for the need of the sinful, the wretched and dying and sin-cursed and disease smitten.

Let the Church return in the glory of God and the power of Christ to the original faith as clearly demonstrated in the New Testament, as perpetuated forever in the Church through the nine gifts of the Holy Spirit, demonstrating beyond controversy that as long as the Holy Spirit is in the Church so long are the gifts of the Holy Spirit, not only present but exercisable through faith. (See 1 Corinthians 12.)

"For to one is given by the Spirit"
First—"The word of wisdom."
Second—"The word of knowledge."
Third—"Faith by the same spirit."
Fourth—"The gifts of healing."
Fifth—"The working of miracles."
Sixth—"To another prophecy."

Seventh—"To another discerning of spirits."

Eighth—"To another divers kinds of tongues."

Ninth—"To another the interpretation of tongues."

The unchanging order of government, spiritual enduement, and ministry of the gifts of the Spirit are further declared as follows; "And God hath set some in the Church, first apostles, secondarily prophets, thirdly, teachers, after that miracles, then gifts of healing, helps, governments, diversities of tongues."

When the Church exercises these gifts then she may condemn Christian Science, Dowieism, or New Thought; then she may condemn every other philosophical cult; then she may condemn Unitarianism, and everything else that you preach against. Though she will not need to. Jesus never did. There were just as many strange philosophies in His day as in ours. The constructive righteousness of Christ, the presence of the living Son of God to save and heal, the revelation to the world of His divine power, will stop the mouths of every 'ism' and manifest one glorious, triumphant, all-embracing power of God through Jesus Christ, His Son, and its everlasting superiority. Neither will you be compelled as you are to glorify doctors, medicines, surgery, and so on, when the greatest physicians on earth have deplored their inability to deliver the world from its curse of sickness. Then you can not only teach the theory of the atonement of our Lord and Savior

Jesus Christ but demonstrate its reality and power to save both soul and body.

All the abstract criticism in the world is powerless to stop the drift from the Churches to Christian Science so long as Christian Science heals the sick and the Church does not. Men demand to be shown. When the authority of Jesus to forgive sins was challenged, He met the challenge with the healing of the palsied man, not with negations and criticisms. He said: "Whether is it easier to say, thy sins be forgiven thee or to say, arise and walk? But that ye may know I say arise and walk." He was too big for abstract criticism. So must the Christian and the Church become.

John G. Lake

15

SPIRITUAL HUNGER

My text tonight, is:

"Blessed are they which do hunger and thirst after righteousness, for they shall be filled." (Matthew 5:6)

Hunger is a mighty good thing. It is the greatest persuader I know of. It is a marvelous mover. Nations have learned that you can do most anything with a populace until they get hungry. But when they get hungry you want to watch out. There is a certain spirit of desperation that accompanies hunger.

I wish we all had it spiritually. I wish to God we were desperately hungry for God. Wouldn't it be glorious? Somebody would get filled before this meeting is over. It would be a strange thing, if we were all desperately hungry for God, if only one or two got filled in a service.

"Blessed are they which do hunger and thirst after righteousness."

Righteousness is just the rightness of God: the rightness of God in your spirit, the rightness of God in your soul, the rightness of God in your body, the rightness of God in your affairs, in your home, in your business, everywhere.

God is an all-around God, His power operates from every side. The artists paint a halo around the head of Jesus to show that there is a radiation of glory from His person. They might just as well put it around his feet or any part of His person. It is the radiant glory of the indwelling God, radiating out through the personality. There is nothing more wonderful than the indwelling of God in the human life. The supremest marvel that God ever performed was when He took possession of those who are hungry.

"Blessed are they which do hunger."

I will guarantee to you that after the crucifixion of Jesus there was a hundred and twenty mighty hungry folks at Jerusalem. I do not believe if they had not been mightily hungry they would have gotten so gloriously filled. It was because they were hungry that they were filled.

We are sometimes inclined to think of God as mechanical; as though God set a date for this event or that to occur. But my opinion is that one of the works of the Holy Ghost is that of preparer. He comes and prepares the heart of men in advance by putting a strange hunger for that event that has been promised by God until it comes to pass.

The more I study history and prophecy the more I am convinced that when Jesus Christ was born into the world He was born in answer to a tremendous heart-cry on the part of the world. The world needed God desperately. They wanted a manifestation of God tremendously, and Jesus Christ as the Deliverer and Savior came in answer to their soul cry.

Daniel says that he was convinced by the study of the books of prophecy, especially that of Jeremiah, that the time had come when they ought to be delivered from their captivity in Babylon. The seventy years was fulfilled but there was no deliverance. So he diligently set his face to pray it into being (Daniel 9).

Here is what I want you to get. If it was going to come to pass mechanically on a certain date, there would not have been any necessity for Daniel to get that awful hunger in his soul, so that he fasted and prayed in sackcloth and ashes, that the deliverance might come.

No sir, God's purposes come to pass when your heart and mine get the real God-cry, and the real God-prayer comes into our spirit, and the real God-yearning gets hold of our nature. Something is going to happen then.

No difference what it may be your soul is coveting or desiring, if it becomes in your life the supreme cry, not the secondary matter, or the third, or the fourth, or fifth or tenth, but the FIRST thing, the supreme desire of your soul, the paramount issue, all the powers and energies of your spirit, of your soul, of your body are reaching out and crying to God for the answer, it is going to come, it is going to come, it is going to come!

I lived in a family where for thirty-two years they never were without an invalid in the home. Before I was twenty-four years of age we had buried four brothers and four sisters, and four other members of the family were dying, hopeless, helpless invalids. I set up my own home, married a beautiful woman. Our first son was born. It was only a short time until I saw that same devilish train of sickness that had followed father's family had come into mine. My wife became an invalid, my son was a sickly child. Out of it all one thing developed in my nature, a cry for deliverance. I did not know anything about the subject of healing, notwithstanding I was a Methodist evangelist. But my heart was crying for deliverance; my soul had come to the place where I had vomited up dependence on man. My father had spent a fortune on the family to no avail, as if there was no stoppage to the train of hell. And let me tell you, there IS NO HUMAN STOPPAGE because the thing is settled deep in the nature of man, too deep for any material remedy to get at it. It takes the Almighty God and the Holy Spirit and the Lord Jesus Christ to get down into the depth of man's nature and find the real difficulty that is there and destroy it.

My brother, I want to tell you, if you are a sinner tonight and away from God, and your heart is longing, and your spirit asking, and your soul crying for God's deliverance, He will be on hand to deliver. You will not have to cry very long until you see that the mountains are being moved, and the angel of deliverance will be there.

I finally got to that place where my supreme cry was for deliverance. Tears were shed for deliverance for three years before the healing of God came to us.

I could hear the cries and groans and sobs, and feel the wretchedness of our family's soul. My heart cried, my soul sobbed, my spirit wept tears. I wanted help. I did not know enough to call directly on God for it. Isn't it a strange thing that men do not have sense enough to have faith in God for all their needs, do not know enough to call directly on God for physical difficulties as well as for spiritual ones? But I did not.

But bless God, one thing matured in my heart, a real hunger. And the hunger of a man's soul must be satisfied, it MUST be satisfied. It is a law of God; that law of God is in the depth of the spirit. God will answer the heart that cries; God will answer the soul that asks. Christ Jesus comes to us with divine assurance and invites us when we are hungry to PRAY, to BELIEVE; to take from the Lord that which our soul covets and our heart asks for.

So one day the Lord of heaven came our way, and in a little while the cloud of darkness, that midnight of hell, that curse of death was lifted, and the light of God shone into our life and into our home, just the same as it existed in other men's lives and other men's homes. We learned the truth of Jesus and was able to apply the divine power of God. We were healed of the Lord.

"Blessed are they which do hunger."

Brethren, begin to pray to get hungry.

At this point I want to tell you a story. I was out on a snow-shoe trip at Sault Ste. Marie, Michigan, where they used to have four and five feet of snow. I tramped for thirty miles on my snow shoes. I was tired and weary. I arrived home and found my wife had gone away to visit, so I went over to my sister's home. I found they were out also. I went into the house and began to look for something to eat. I was I was nearly starved. I found a great big sort of cake that looked like corn broad. It was still quite warm and it smelled good. I ate it all. I thought it was awful funny stuff, and it seemed to have lumps in it. I did not just understand the combination, and I was not much of a cook. About the time I had finished it my sister and her husband came in. She said, "My you must be awful tired and hungry." I said, "I was but I just found a corn cake and ate the whole thing." She said, "My goodness, John, you did not eat that?" I said, "What was it, Irene?" "Why that was a kind of cow bread, we grind up cobs and all." You see it depends on the character and degree of your hunger. Things taste mighty good to a hungry man.

If you wanted to confer a peculiar blessing on men at large, it would not be to give them but to make them hungry, and then every thing that came their way would taste everlastingly good.

I love to tell this story because it is the story of a hungry man. A short time after I went to South Africa and God had begun to work very marvelously in the city of Johannesburg. A butcher who lived in the suburbs was advised by his physicians that he had developed such a tubercular state he might not live more than nine months. He wanted to make provision that his family be cared for after he was gone, so he bought a farm and undertook to develop it that when he died his family would have a means of existence.

One day he received a letter from friends at Johannesburg, telling of the coming of what they spoke of as "the American Brethren," and of the wonderful things that were taking place. Of how so-and-so, a terrible drunkard, had been converted; of his niece who had been an invalid in a wheel chair for five years, had been healed of God; how one of his other relatives had been baptized in the Holy Ghost and was speaking in tongues; other friends and neighbors had been baptized and healed of the powerful change that had come in the community, and all the marvels a vigorous work for God produces.

Dan Von Vuuren took the letter, crawled under an African thorn tree. He spread the letter out before God, and began to discuss it with the Lord. He said, "God in heaven, if you could come to Mr. So-and-so, a drunkard, and deliver him from his sin and save his soul and put the joy of God in him; if you could come to this niece of mine, save her soul and heal her body and send her out to be a blessing instead of a weight and burden upon her friends; if you could come to so-and-so, so they were baptized in the Holy Ghost and speak in tongues; Lord, if you can do these things at Johannesburg, you can do something for me too." And he knelt down, put his face to the ground, and cried to God that God would do something for him. And don't forget it, friends, I have a conviction that that morning Dan Von Vuuren was so stirred by the reading of that letter that His desire to be made whole got bigger than anything else in his consciousness. His heart reached for God, and bless God, that morning his prayer went through to heaven and God came down into his life. In ten minutes he took all the breath he wanted; the pain was gone, the tuberculosis had disappeared, he was a whole man.

But that was not all, he not only received a great physical healing, but God had literally come in and taken possession of the man's life until he did not understand himself any more. In telling me he said, "Brother, a new prayer from heaven was born in my spirit. I had prayed for my wife's salvation for eighteen years, but I could never pray through. But that morning I prayed through. It was all done when I got to the house. She stood and looked at me for two minutes, until it dawned in her soul that I was gloriously healed of God. She never asked a question as to how it took place, but fell on her knees, threw her hands up to heaven, and said, 'Pray for me. Dan, for God's sake, pray for me. I must find God today,' and God came to that soul."

He has eleven children, splendid young folks. The mother and he went to praying and inside of a week the whole household of thirteen had been baptized in the Holy Ghost. He went to his brother's farm; told the wonder of what God has done; prayed through

182

and in a little while nineteen families were baptized in the Holy Ghost.

God so filled his life with His glory that one morning God said to him, "Go to Pretoria. I am going to send you to different members of Parliament." He was admitted into the presence of Premier Louis Botha. Botha told me about it afterwards. He said, "Lake, I had known Van Vurren from the time he was a boy. I had known him as a reckless, rollicking fellow. But that man came into my office and stood ten feet from my desk. I looked up, and before he commenced to speak, I began to shake and rattle on my chair. I knelt down, I had to put my head under the desk and cry to God." Why he looked like God; and talked like God. He had the majesty of God. He was superhumanly wonderful. Then he went to the office of the Secretary of State, then to the Secretary of the Treasury. Almost the same thing took place in every instance. For eighteen days God kept him going from this one to that one; lawyers, judges and officials in the land, until every high official in the land knew there was a God and a Christ and a Savior, and a baptism of the Holy Ghost, because Von Vuuren has really hungered after God.

"Blessed are they which do hunger."

I was sitting here tonight before the meeting and began reading an old sermon I preached to a men's club at Spokane, Washington eight years ago, entitled "The Calling of the Soul." In it I observed I recounted the story of the original people who came to the Parham School in 1900, and whom in answer to the cry of their soul God came and baptized them in the Holy Ghost. All the Apostolic Faith Churches, and Missions, and Assemblies of God, and other movements are the result.

I knew Brother Parham's wife and his sister-in-law, Lillian Thistleweight. She was the woman that brought the light of God for real sanctification to my heart. It was not her preaching or her words. I sat in Fred Bosworth's home one night before Fred thought of preaching the gospel. I listened to that woman telling of the Lord God and His love and sanctifying grace and power, and what real holiness was. It was not her arguments or logic; it was herself; it was the divine holiness that came from her soul; it was the living Spirit of God that came out of the woman's life. I sat way back in the room, as far way as I could get. I was self satisfied, doing well in the world, prosperous with all the accompaniments that go with successful life. But that night, my heart got so hungry that I fell on my knees, and those who were present will tell you yet that they had never heard anybody pray as I prayed. Bosworth said long afterward, "Lake, there is one instance that I shall always remember in your life; that was the night you prayed in my home until the rafters shook, until God came down, until the fire struck, until our souls melted, until God came in and sanctified our hearts." All the devils in hell and out of hell could not make me believe there is not a real sanctified experience in Jesus Christ; when God comes in and makes your heart pure and takes self out of your nature, and gives you divine triumph over sin and self, blessed be the Name of the Lord!

"Blessed are they which do hunger."

Beloved, pray to get hungry.

Coming back to Dan Von Vuuren. For several years before I left Africa he went up and down the land like a burning fire. Everywhere he went sinners were saved, sick were healed, men and women were baptized in the Holy Ghost, until he set the outlying districts on fire with the power of God; and he is going still.

Here is a point I want to bring to you. As I talked with Lillian Thistleweight, I observed the one supreme thing in that woman's soul was the consciousness of holiness. She said, "Brother, that is what we prayed for, that is what the baptism brought to us."

Later Brother Parham was preaching in Texas. A colored man came into his meeting by the name of Seymour. In a hotel in Chicago he related his experience to Brother Tom and myself. I want you to see the hunger in that colored man's soul. He said he was a waiter in a restaurant and preaching to a Church of colored people. He knew God as Savior, as the sanctifier. He knew the power of God to heal. But as he listened to Parham he became convinced of a bigger thing, the baptism of Holy Ghost. He went on to Los Angeles without receiving it, but he said he was determined to preach all of God he knew to the people. He said, "Brother, before I met Parham, such a hunger to have more of God was in my heart that I prayed for five hours a day for two and a half years. I got to Los Angeles, and when I got there the hunger was not less but more. I prayed, God, what can I do? And the Spirit said, pray more. But Lord, I am praying five hours a day now. I increased my hours of prayer to seven, and prayed on for a year and a half more. I prayed God to give me what Parham preached, the real Holy Ghost and fire with tongues and love and power of God, like the apostles had." There are better things to he had in spiritual life but they must be sought out with faith and prayer. I want to tell you God Almighty had such a hunger in that man's heart that when the fire of God came it glorified him. I do not believe that any other man in modern times had a more wonderful deluge of God in his life that God gave to that dear fellow. Brother Seymour preached to my congregation, to ten thousand people, when the glory and power of God was upon his spirit, when men shook and trembled and cried to God. God was in him.

"Blessed are they which do hunger for they shall be filled."

I wonder what we are hungering for? Have we a real divine hunger, something our soul is asking for? If you have God will answer; God will answer. By every law of of the Spirit that men know, it is due to come. It will come! Bless God, it will come. It will come in more ways than you ever dreamed of. God is not confined to manifesting himself in tongues and interpretation alone. His life in man is rounded.

When I was a lad, I accompanied my father on a visit to the office of John A. McCall, the great insurance man. We were taken to McCall's office in his private elevator. It was the first time I had ever been in a great office building and had ridden on an elevator, and I remember holding my breath until the thing stopped. Then we stepped into his office, the most beautiful office I had ever beheld. The rugs were so thick I was afraid I would go through the floor when I stepped on them. His desk was a marvel, pure mahogany, and on the top of his desk, inlaid in mother of pearl, was his name, written in script. It was so magnificent that in my boyish soul I said, "I am going to have an office just like this and a desk like that with my name on it when I am a man."

I did not know how much of an asking it was in my nature, and it seemed sometimes that it had drifted away, until I was in my thirtieth year, I was invited to come to Chicago to join an association of men who were establishing a Life Insurance Association. They said, "Lake, we want you to manage this Association." We dickered about the matter for three weeks until they came to my terms, and finally the president said, "Step into this office until we show you something. We have a surprise for you." And I stepped into an office just exactly the duplicate of John A. McCall's office, and there in the center was a desk of pure mahogany, and instead of the name of John A. McCall, it was John G. Lake, in mother of pearl. I had never spoken of that soul desire to a person in the world.

Friends, there is a something in the call of the soul that is creative. It brings things to pass. Don't you know that when the supreme desire of your heart goes out to God, all the spiritual energy of your nature and the powers of God that come to you begin to concentrate and work along that certain line, and form and form, and there comes by the unconscious creative exercise of faith into being that which your soul calls for. That is the creative action of faith, you and God together working out and evidencing the power of creative desire.

Tongues and Interpretation, by Mrs. Jas. Wilson and Brother Myreen:

"Ye shall receive the desire of your heart if you come before Me in prayer and supplication, for I am a God that answers my children. Go ye forward in the battle for I shall be with you and fulfill the desire of your heart, Yes, pray that ye may become hungry.

"Call and I shall answer, for I am a God that hears. I shall answer your call. Come before Me; humble yourselves before My feet, and I shall answer your call.

"Be ye diligent before Me, and pray, yea, be ye in prayer and supplication, for ye are living in the last days, and my Spirit shall not always strive with men.

But ye that humble yourselves before Me will know I shall be your God. I shall strengthen you on the right hand and on the left, and ye shall understand and know that I am your living God."

When Moses stood at the Red Sea he tried to back out of that relationship God was establishing and tried to throw the responsibility back on God. He was overwhelmed. It was too marvelous. Surely God must not have meant it. But God knew. When he began to recognize himself as an individual and God as another it was offensive to God. He thought he could back up and pray for God to do something for him the same as God used to do in the old relationship. He could not do it. When he got down to pray, in the mind of God the idea of Moses not backing water and getting out of that close place, that inner relationship, that divine symphony of Moses' soul and God's, it was offensive to Him. And God said,

"Wherefore criest thou unto me?"

In other words, shut up your praying. Get up out of there.

"Lift thou up, thy rod, and stretch out thine hand over the sea, and DIVIDE IT" (Exodus 14:15-16).

God did not say, Moses you stretch forth your hand, and I will divide the sea. But He said:

"Stretch out thine hand over the sea, and divide it."

Moses, you and I are one, stretch forth your hand and divide the sea. You have all there is of me and I

189

have all there is of you. We are one and indivisible. God and man becomes one. The heart of man, the mind of man, the soul of man enters into God, and God into him. The divine fires of the eternal Christ, by the Holy Ghost, come from heaven, and the lightnings of Jesus flash through the life, bless God, and the power of Christ invigorates and manifests and demonstrates through that relationship.

God revealed that to my soul in the days when I first went to Africa, within six weeks after my feet touched the soil, and before God had given me a white Church to preach in. I said, "Lord, when you give me a Church in which to preach this gospel, I will preach the highest and holiest thing God's Spirit reveals to my heart. I do not care if anybody else believes it or sees it; I am going to preach the vision the Son of God puts in my soul."

Bless God, He put the high vision of the glorified Christ and the glorified Christian: not a man simply saved from sin, but a man saved from his sins, sanctified by His power, infilled with His Spirit, re-created with and in Jesus Christ, one in nature, character and substance. My heart began to preach it, and my mouth gave the message, and my soul sent forth the word, and my spirit called such that wanted to be that character of man to come to the feet of the Son of God, and receive His blessing and receive His power. And, beloved, I tell you that in all the modern world there never was another hundred and twenty-five preachers who went out of a Church to proclaim the power of God with greater power than that first hundred and twenty-five men did. The thing that was in my soul fired Dan Von Vuuren's soul and kindled the faith of the people. Wherever it spread it set men on fire for God.

Friends, we need a coming up into God. This Church, and the Church around the world needs to come up into God. We have been traveling around in a circle, and digging our noses in the ground, and we have had our eyes on the ground, instead of up in the clouds, instead of up at the throne. Look up to the glorified One! If you want to see His bleeding hands, look to heaven where He is to see them. Do not look back to Calvary to see them. He is the risen, regnant, glorified Son of God in heaven, with all power and all authority; with the keys of hell and of death! He is the divine authority, the eternal overcoming, manifestation of God in Heaven. And you and the regnant, glorified Christ as one, are the divine manifestation of God. Come up to the Throne, dear ones. Let the Throne life, and the Throne love, and the Throne power and the Throne Spirit, and the Holy Ghost in heaven possess you, and you will be a new man in Christ Jesus! And your tread will be the march of the conqueror and your song the song of victory, and your crown the crown of glory, and your power the power of God.

16

BEHOLD, I GIVE YOU POWER

"When He was come down from the mountain, great multitudes followed Him, and behold, there came a leper and worshipped Him, saying, Lord, if thou wilt, thou canst make me clean" (Matthew 8:1-2).

That man knew that Jesus had the power to heal him, but he did not know it was God's will, and that Jesus had committed Himself to the healing of mankind. If he had known he would have said, "Lord, heal me."

It is always God's will to heal. Our faith may fail. My faith failed to the extent that unless someone else had gone under my life and prayed for me, I would have died. But God was just as willing to heal me as He could be. It was my faith that broke down. God is willing, just as willing to heal as He is to save. HEALING IS A PART OF SALVATION. It is not separate from salvation. Healing was purchased by the blood of Jesus. This Book always connects salvation and healing.

David said: "Bless the Lord, O my soul, and forget not all His benefits: Who forgiveth all thine iniquities; Who healeth all thy diseases" (Psalm 103:2-3).

There never has been a man in the world who was

converted, and was sick at the same time, who might not have been healed if he had believed God for it. But he was not instructed in faith to believe God for healing.

Suppose two men came to the altar. One is sick and lame; the other is a sinner. Suppose they knelt at the altar together. The sinner says, "I want to find the Lord." Everyone in the house will immediately lend the love of their heart and the faith of their soul to help him touch God. But the lame fellow says, "I have a lame leg" or "my spine is injured. I want healing." Instead of everybody lending their love and faith in the same way to that man, everybody puts up a question mark.

That comes because of the fact we are instructed on the Word of God concerning the salvation of the soul, but our education concerning sickness and His desire and willingness to heal had been neglected. We have gone to the eighth or the tenth grade or the university on the subject of salvation, but on the subject of healing we are in the ABC class.

"Jesus put forth His hand, and touched him, saying, I will: be thou clean" (Matthew 8:3). Did He ever say anything in the world but "I will," or did He ever say, "I cannot heal you because it is not the will of God," or "I cannot heal you because you are being purified by this sickness," or "I cannot heal you because you are glorifying God in this sickness?" There is no such instance in the Book.

On the other hand we are told "He healed ALL

that came to Him." Never a soul ever applied to God for salvation or healing that Jesus did not save and heal! Did you ever think what calamity it might have been if a man had come to Jesus once and said, "Lord, save me," and the Lord had said, "No, I cannot save you." Every man forevermore would have a question mark as to whether or not God would save him. There would not be a universal confidence as there is today.

Suppose Jesus had ever said to a sick man, "No, I cannot heal you." You would have the same doubt about healing. The world would have settled back and said, "Well, it may be God's will to heal that man or that woman, but I do not know whether or not it is His will to heal me."

Jesus Christ did not leave us in doubt about God's will, but when the Church lost her faith in God, she began to teach the people that maybe it was not God's will to heal them. So the Church introduced the Phrase, "If it be Thy will" concerning healing. But Jesus "healed all that came to Him" (Matthew 4:23; Luke 9:6; Luke 9:11).

Notice what it says in Isaiah 35, "He will come and save you. The the eyes of the blind shall be opened, and the ears of the deaf shall be unstopped. Then shall the lame man shall leap as an hart, and the tongue of the dumb shall sing." Salvation and healing connected!

"That it might be fulfilled which was spoken by Isaiah the prophet, saying, Himself took our infirmities and bare our sicknesses" (Matthew 8:17).

And lest we might be unmindful of that great fact that he "bare our sicknesses and carried our sorrows," Peter emphasizes it by saying, "Who his own self bare our sins in His own body on the tree, that we being dead to sins, should live unto righteousness: by whose stripes ye were healed" (1 Peter 2:24). Not "by whose stripes ye are healed," but "by whose stripes ye were healed." The only thing that is necessary is to BELIEVE GOD. God's mind never needs to act for a man's salvation. He gave the Lord and Savior Jesus Christ to die for you. God cannot go any farther in expressing His will in His desire to save man. The only thing that is necessary is to believe God. There is salvation by blood. There is salvation by power that actually comes of God into a man's life. The blood provided the power. Without the blood there would have been no power. Without the sacrifice there would have never been any glory. Salvation by blood, salvation by power.

The Church in general is very clear in her faith on the subject of salvation through the sacrifice of the Lord and Savior Jesus Christ. The Christian world in general, regardless of their personal state of salvation, has a general faith and belief of the Lord and Savior Jesus Christ for the salvation of the world. But they are ever in doubt and very inexperienced on the power of God.

"When He was come down from the mountain, great multitudes followed Him. And, behold, there came a leper and worshipped Him, saying, Lord, if thou wilt, thou canst make me clean. And Jesus put forth His hand, and touched him, saying, I will: be thou clean. And immediately his leprosy was cleansed. And Jesus saith unto him, See thou tell no man; but go thy way, shew thyself to the priest, and offer the gift that Moses commanded, for a testimony unto them" (Matthew 8:1-4).

Did you ever stop to think that they have no medical remedy for the real things that kill folks? Typhoid fever: Fill the patient with a tankful of medicine and he will go right on for twenty-one days.

In 1913, I was in Chicago in a big meeting when I received a telegram from the hospital in Detroit, saying, "Your son, Otto, is sick with typhoid fever. If you want to see him, come." I rushed for a train, and when I arrived I found him in a ward. I told the man in charge I would like a private room for him so I could get a chance to pray for him. Well, God smote that thing in five minutes. I stayed with him for a couple of days until he was up and walking around. He went along for four or five weeks, and one day, to my surprise, I got another telegram telling me he had a relapse of typhoid. So I went back again. This time there was no sunburst of God like the first time. Everything was as cold as steel, and my, I was so conscious of the power of the devil. I could not pray audibly, but I sat down by his bed and shut my teeth, and I said in my soul, "Now, Mr. Devil, go to it. You kill him if you can." And I sat there five days and nights. He did not get healing the second time instantly. It was healing by process because of the fact my soul took hold on God. I sat with my teeth shut, and I never left his bedside until it was done.

You may be healed like a sunburst of God today, and tomorrow, the next week or the next month when you want healing you may have to take it on the slow process. The action of God is not always the same because the conditions are not always the same.

In the life of Jesus people were instantly healed. I believe Jesus has such a supreme measure of the Spirit that when He put His hands on a man he was filled and submerged in the Holy Ghost, and the diseases withered-out and vanished.

But, beloved, you and I use the measure of the Spirit that we possess. And if we haven't got as much of God as Jesus had then you pray for a man today, and you get a certain measure of healing, but he is not entirely well. The only thing to do is to pray for him tomorrow, and let him get some more, and keep on until he is well.

That is where people blunder. They will pray for a day or two, and then they quit. You pray and keep on day by day and minister to your sick until they are well. One of the things that has discredited healing is that evangelists will hold meetings, and hundreds of sick will come and be prayed for. In a great meeting like that you get a chance to pray once and do not see them again. You pray for ten people, and as a a rule you will find that one or two or three are absolutely healed, but the others are only half healed, or quarter healed or have only a little touch of healing. It is just the same with salvation. You bring ten to the altar. One is saved and is clear in his soul. Another may come for a week, and another for a month before he is clear in his soul. The difference is not with God. The difference is inside the man. His consciousness has not opened up to God.

Every law of the Spirit that applies to salvation applies to healing likewise.

"And when Jesus was entered into Capernaum, there came unto Him a centurion, beseeching Him, and saying, Lord, my servant lieth at home sick of the palsy, grievously tormented. And Jesus saith unto him, I will come and heal him. The centurion answered and said, Lord, I am not worthy that thou shouldst come under my roof: but speak the word only, and my servant shall be healed" (Matthew 8:5-8).

Here is healing at a distance. That centurion understood divine authority, and the same divine authority is vested in the Christian, for Jesus is the pattern Christian.

"For I am a man under authority, having soldiers under me: and I say to this man, Go, and he goeth; and to another, Come, and he cometh and to my servant, Do this, and he doeth it" (Matthew 8:9).

The same divine authority that was vested in Jesus is vested BY JESUS in every Christian soul. Jesus made provision for the Church of Jesus Christ to go on forever and do the same as He did, and to keep on doing them forever. That is what is the matter with the Church. The Church has lost faith in that truth. The result, they went on believing He could save them from sin, but the other great range of Christian life was left to the doctors and the devil or anything else. And the Church will never be a real Church, in the real power of the living God again, until she comes back again to the original standard where Jesus was.

Jesus said, "Behold, I give you authority." What authority? "Over unclean spirits to cast them out, and to heal all manner of sickness and all manner of disease" (Matthew 10:1). Jesus has vested that authority in you. You say, "Well, Lord, we understand the authority that is in your Word, but we haven't the power." But Jesus said, "Ye shall receive power, after that the Holy Ghost is come upon you" (Acts 1:8).

Now the Holy Ghost is come upon every Christian in a measure. It is a question of degree. There are degrees of the measure of the Spirit of God in men's lives. The BAPTISM OF THE HOLY SPIRIT is a greater measure of the Spirit of God, but every man has a degree of the Holy Spirit in his life. You have. It is the Spirit in your life that gives faith in God, that makes you a blessing to other people. It is the Holy Spirit that is out-breathed in your soul that touches another soul and moves them for God. Begin right where you are and let God take you along the Christian life as far as you like.

"When Jesus heard it, He marveled and said to

them that followed Verily, I say unto you, I have not found so great faith, no, not in Israel" (Matthew 8:10).

Jesus always commended faith when He met it. Jesus did not always meet faith. All the people who came to Jesus did not possess that order of faith. They had faith that IF THEY GOT TO JESUS they would be healed. But here is a man who says, "Speak the word only, and my servant shall be healed."

Then you remember the case of the man at the Pool of Bethesda. He did not even ask to be healed. As he lay there Jesus walked up to him and said, "Wilt thou be made whole?" The poor fellow went on to say that when the water was troubled he had no one to put him in, but while waiting another stepped in ahead of him, But Jesus said unto him, "Arise, take up thy bed and walk." He was made whole. Afterward Jesus met him and said, "Behold thou art made whole: sin no more, lest a worse thing come unto thee" (John 5:14).

Most of sickness is the result of sin. That is the answer to the individual who sins. For thousands of years men have been sinning, and in consequence of their sin, they are diseased in their bodies. This will give you an idea. Scientists tell us there are tubercular germs in 90% of the population. The only difference is that when people are in a healthy state, the germs do not get a chance to manifest themselves. I am trying to show the intimacy between sin and sickness. Not necessarily the sin of the individual. It may never be the sin of the individual.

In the records of the Lake and Graham family away back, tuberculosis was never known to them, until it appeared in my sister. My sister accompanied me to Africa and she became so ill that when I got to Cape Town we had to wait until her strength returned. God healed her.

Regarding people being healed at a distance, we receive telegrams from all over the world. Distance is no barrier to God. The United States has just finished the building of the greatest wireless station in the world. They send messages that register almost instantly, ten thousand miles away. Well, all right, when your HEART strikes God in faith, it will register there wherever that individual is just that quick. All the discoveries of later years such as telegraph, telephone wireless and that sort of thing are just the common laws that Christians have practiced all their lives.

Nobody ever knelt down and prayed, but that the instant they touched God their soul registered in Jesus Christ in Glory, and the answer came back to the soul. Christians have that experience every day. The wise world has begun to observe that these laws are applicable in the natural realm. I asked Marconi once how he got his first idea for the wireless, He replied he got it from watching an exhibition of telepathy in a cheap theatre.

The prayer of the heart reaches God. Jesus replied to the leper, "I will: be thou clean." The next was the centurion's servant. The centurion said "You do not need to come to my house. You SPEAK THE WORD ONLY and my servant shall be healed." And in the soul of Jesus He said, "Be healed." Distance is no barrier to God. Distance makes no difference. The Spirit of God will go as far as your love reaches. Love is the medium that conveys the Spirit of God to another soul anywhere on God's earth.

This is what takes place when you pray. The Spirit of God comes upon you and bathes your soul, and a shaft of it reaches out and touches that soul over there, If you had an instrument that was fine enough to photograph spirit, you would discover this is done.

Is it not a marvelous thing that God has chosen us to be co-laborers with Him, and He takes us into partnership to do all that He is doing? Jesus Christ at the Throne of God desires the blessing of you and me, and out of His holy heart the Spirit comes, and the soul is filled, and we cannot tell how or why.

I have known thousands of people to be healed who have never seen my face. They send a request for prayer, we pray, and never hear anything more about them sometimes, unless a friend or a neighbor or someone comes and tells us about them. Sometimes someone sends in a request for them. They will tell you they do not know what happened. They just got well. But you know why. That is the wonderful power there is in the Christian life, and that is the wonderful cooperation that the Lord Jesus has arranged between His own soul and the soul of the Christian. That is the Church which is his body.

17

THE CALLING OF THE SOUL

If I were to choose a subject for the thought in my soul tonight, I would choose "The Calling of the Soul."

Someone has given us this little saying that has become prevalent among many people. "My own shall come to me." Jesus framed that thought in different words. He said: "He that hungers and thirsts after righteousness shall be filled." It is the same law. "Blessed are they that hunger and thirst after righteousness, for they shall be filled."

RIGHTEOUSNESS is simply God's rightness. God's rightness in a man's soul, God's rightness in a man's spirit, God's rightness in a man's body. In order that man may be right or righteous, God imparts to man the power of His Spirit. That Spirit contains such marvelous and transforming grace that when received into the nature of man, the marvelous process of regeneration is set in motion and man becomes thereby a new creature in Christ Jesus.

The deepest call of our nature is the one that will find the speediest answer. People pray, something happens. If they pray again something still deeper occurs within their nature, and they find a new prayer. The desire is obtained.

In my ministry in South Africa, I had a preacher by the name of Van Vuuren. That name means "fire." Van Vuuren had been a butcher in the city of Johannesburg and was given up to die of consumption. His physician said to him: "You have only one year to live." So he gave up his business and went down into the country to develop a farm, that his family might be able to support themselves.

After he left the city many were baptized in the Holy Spirit and healed, and so forth, and his friends wrote him a letter and "So-and-so, who was sick, has been healed; So-and-so, your niece, has been baptized in the Holy Spirit and is speaking in tongues by the power of God; So-and-so has been blessed of God," and so on.

Van Vuuren took the letter and went out into the fields and got down under a thorn tree and spread the letter out before God. Then he began to pray: "God, if you can do these things for the people at Johannesburg, you can do something for me. I have been a Christian for eighteen years, and I have prayed and prayed for certain things which have not come to pass. God, if others can be baptized in the Holy Ghost, surely I can; if other's hearts are made pure by the power of God, the power that made theirs pure can make mine pure also; if others have been healed, then you can heal me."

As he thus gave himself to God, and opened his soul to heaven, suddenly the Spirit came upon him and he became the most transformed creature I ever knew.

God moved into the man. For eighteen days he walked as though overshadowed by the Spirit of God, God talking continuously to his soul, directing him to this one and that one, judges and lawyers, statesmen and physicians, rich and poor. When he would reach them the Spirit of God would pour forth through his soul such messages of God that in many cases they fell down and wept.

This is the point of the story I wanted you to get. He said for eighteen years he had prayed for the real conversion and transformation of his wife, and it had not come to pass. But that morning after the Lord had baptized him in the Holy Ghost a new prayer came into his heart, a new depth had been touched in the man's nature, and from that great inner depth flowed out to God a cry that had been going out from his soul for years. But that morning the cry of God touched the soul of his wife, and before he reached the house she had given her heart to God. In three months all his family, his wife, eleven children and himself, had been baptized in the Holy Spirit.

The desire of which Jesus spoke of (for when He spoke of desire, He spoke of this same call of the soul) was not the simple attitude of the outer man. Certainly it included it. Perhaps the desire in the beginning was simply that of the mind, but as the days and years passed, and the desire ability of obtaining grew in the soul, it became a call of the deepest depth of the man's nature. And that is the character of desire that Jesus spoke of when He said: "Blessed are they that hunger and thirst after righteousness, for they shall be filled."

The spiritual action that takes place within the nature of man, that strong desire for God, His ways, His love, His knowledge, His power, causes everything else, perhaps unconsciously to himself, to become secondary.

Politicians talk about a paramount issue. That is the issue that stands out by itself above all others and is the greatest and largest and of most interest to the nation. It is the paramount issue.

The soul has its paramount issue, and when the desire of your heart is intensified so that it absorbs all your energies, then the time of its fulfillment is not far away. That is the desire that brings the answer. It is creative desire.

A woman testified in my hearing one day to this fact. She had been pronounced hopeless and was going blind. No human remedy could do her any good. Someone opened to her in a dim way the possibility of seeing through the power of God. She was not very well taught, but she said this: "That every day for four years she gave up two and one-half hours absolutely to expressing the desire of her soul for real sight. Not only expressing it in words, but calling the power of God to her that would recreate in her the function of sight in her eyes and make her see." At the end of four or four and a half years she said: "My eyes are as well as they ever were."

That is the reward of persistence, of a desire toward God. Your nature may have sent out just as deep a cry to God as my nature has, and still is doing. Is the cry to God continuous? Gradually as the forces of life concentrate themselves in line with that strong desire, the Spirit of God is operating through your heart, is being directed by that desire and concentrated on a particular line, intensifying every day because of the continuous desire of the soul to possess. The effect of that concentration of the Spirit of God on that soul is that by the grace of God there is brought to your soul all the elements necessary to formulate and create and fulfill the desire of your heart, and one morning the soul awakens to discover that it has become the possessor of the desired object.

Jesus started men on the true foundation. Many simply desire health, others temporal blessings. Both are good and proper, but bless God, Jesus started the soul at the proper point, to first desire RIGHTEOUSNESS, the righteousness of God, to become a possessor of the Kingdom. "Seek ye first," said Jesus, "the Kingdom of God and His righteousness, and all these things shall be added unto you."

Jesus was bringing forth and establishing in the world a new character, a character that would endure forever, a soul quality that would never fail, a faith that knew no possibility of defeat. In establishing such a character Jesus saw that the character could only be established in the depth of a Man's being, in the very spirit of his being. Then when once the soul was grounded in the paths of righteousness, then all the activities of the nature would be along righteous lines, and in harmony with the laws of God.

God has a call in His own Spirit. If we study our own spirit we will understand the nature of God. The call of the Spirit of God is the call of righteousness, the call of truth, the call of love, the call of power, the call of faith.

I met a young man on one occasion who seemed to me to be the most blessed man, in some ways, of all the men I had ever met. I observed he was surrounded by a circle of friends of men or women, the deepest and truest it had ever been my privilege to know. One day I said to him: "What is the secret of this circle of friends that you possess, and the manner in which you seem to bind them to you." He replied, "Lake, my friendships are the result of the call of the soul. My soul has called for truth and righteousness, for holiness, for grace, for strength, for soundness of mind, for the power of God, and the call has reached this one, and this one and this one, and brought them to me."

Over in Topeka, Kansas, in the year 1900, one morning a man stepped off the train, walked up the street, and as he walked up a particular street he stopped in front of a large fine dwelling, and said to himself, "This is the house." A gentlemen who happened to be out of sight around the building said,

"What about the house?" and this story came out. He said: "For years I have been praying God for a certain work of God among Christians known as the Baptism of the Holy Ghost. In my researches I have visited every body of Christian people in this country that I knew of that claimed to be possessors of the baptism, but as I visited and examined their experiences and compared it with the Word of God, I became convinced that none of them possessed the Baptism of the Holy Ghost as it is recorded and demonstrated in the New Testament."

He said one day as he prayed, the Spirit of the Lord said, "Go to Topeka, Kansas." As he prayed he observed in the Spirit a certain house, and the Lord said, "I will give you that house, and in it the Baptism of the Holy Ghost will fall."

So he took the train and came to Topeka, walked down the street, and exclaimed as he passed by, "This is the house," and the voice around the corner replied, "What about it?" When the man had heard his story, he told him he was the owner of the house; that it had been closed for years. He asked him what he wanted it for, and he replied that he was going to start a Christian school. The owner said, "Have you any money?" He replied, "No." He said, "All right, you can have the house without money."

About an hour later a little Quaker lady came down the street, hesitated and looked around and said, "This is the house, but there is no one living there." After a struggle with her soul she went up and rang the door bell and the first gentlemen answered the bell and asked what she wanted. She said: "I live over in the country at such a place. As I prayed, the Spirit told me to come here to this house." He said, "Who are you?" She replied, "Just an unknown Christian woman." He said: "What have you been praying about?" She said, "About the Baptism of the Holy Ghost."

Beloved, in three weeks eighteen persons were brought to that house. They formed a little company and began to pray. The company grew to thirty-six. On New Years night, 1900, the Spirit fell on that company, and the first one was baptized in the Holy Ghost, and in a few weeks practically the whole company had been baptized in the Holy Ghost. And from there is spread over the world.

Yesterday morning a woman came to my healing rooms, a stranger in the city. She said, "I have been praying for healing and asking God to show me where I could be healed. I heard of friends in Chicago who pray for the sick, and I visited them, but when I arrived, the Spirit said, 'Not here.'" She said, "I bought a ticket and was about to take a train back home, but as I sat in the station I was approached by a little lady on crutches, and pitying her, I turned to speak a kind word to her. While conversing with her I saw she was a Christian of a deep nature, rarely found. I told her my story." She said, "Oh, I know where the Lord wants you to go. The Lord wants you to go to Spokane, Washington" (3000 miles from

Chicago). She asked her if she knew anybody in Spokane, and the lady replied, "Why yes, I know Mr. Lake, I used to nurse in his home years ago."

I prayed for her, and told her the thing to do was to came in for ministry every day until she was well. She said she would. This morning I received a call on the telephone, and she said, "I am not coming up to the healing rooms." I said, "Oh, is that the kind of individual you are? The one that comes once and gets nothing." "No," she said, "I came once and got something, and I do not need to come back. I am healed, and I am going home."

There is a call of faith in this Church, that is reaching away out, far out and in unaccountable ways. Away at the other end the Spirit of God is revealing truth to this soul and that soul, and they are moving into this life, and coming into unity with this Church.

Is there a note of despair in your heart? Have you not obtained the thing your soul covets? Have you desired to be like that sinless, unselfish, sickless One? God will answer the call of your soul. You shall have your hearts desire. But before that call becomes answerable is must be the paramount call of your being. It is when it becomes the paramount issue of the soul that the answer comes. Jesus knew. That is the reason He said, "Blessed are they that hunger and thirst after righteousness, for they shall be filled." There is not a doubt about it. All the barriers of your nature will go down before the desire of the soul. All the obstacles that ever were will disappear before the desire of you soul. All the diseases that ever existed in your life will disappear before the desire of your soul, when that desire becomes the one great purpose and prayer of your heart.

I love to think of one great soul: he was not a great Christian, but he was a great soul. He was the son of a Church of England clergyman, and came to South Africa, thinking he might get his system back to a normal state of health. He came to the SSS diamond mines at Kimberley and took a pick and shovel and worked with them long enough to understand diamonds. Indeed, he studied diamonds until he knew more about them than any other man in the world. Then he went to studying Africa, until one paramount desire grew up in his soul. He said, "I will plant the British flag across the continent." Eventually, this is what he did. He told me that in the beginning his vision extended to the Vaal River, then to the Zambezi and then across the trackless desert. He also planned a railroad six thousand miles long. John Cecil Rhodes died before he could fully bring to pass the paramount issue of his soul!

"Blessed are they that hunger and thirst after righteousness."

Oh, if I had one gift, or one desire that I would bestow on you, more than all others, I would bestow upon you the hunger for God.

"Blessed are they that hunger." Hunger is the best thing that ever came into a man's life. Hunger is hard to endure. It is the call of the nature for something that you do not possess. The thing that will satisfy the demands of the nature and the hunger of a man's soul is the call of his nature for the Spirit of life that will generate in him the abundant love of God.

Years ago I was one of a family of which some member was an invalid in the house for thirty-two consecutive years. During that time we buried four brothers and four sisters. A call arose in my nature to God for something to stay that tide of sickness and death. *Materia medica* had utterly failed. One after another the tomb stones were raised. The call arose in my soul for something from God that would stem the tide and turn it backward.

Nothing else but healing could have come to my life, no other thing but the knowledge of it. God had to bring from the furthest ends of Australia the man who brought to my soul the message of God and the manifestation of His power that satisfied my heart. And healing by the power of God became a fact to me.

We live that our souls may grow. The development of the soul is the purpose of existence. God Almighty is trying to obtain some decent association for Himself. By His grace He is endeavoring to have us grow up in His knowledge and likeness to that stature where as sons of God we will comprehend something of His love, of His nature, of His power, of His purpose, and be big enough to give back to God what a son should give to a great Father: the reverence, the love, the affection that comes from the understanding of the nobleness and greatness of His purpose.

Great Britain produced two marvelous statesmen, a father and his son. They are known in history as the old Pitt and the young Pitt. The young Pitt was as great a statesman as his father. The son grew to that largeness where, catching the vision of his great father his soul arose to it, and he became his father's equal. As I walked through the House of Commons I came across the statues of the old and young Pitt. I have forgotten the inscription at the bottom of the elder Pitt's statue, but at the base of the son's statue were these words: "My father, the greatest man I ever knew." Do you see the call of his soul for his father's largeness, for his father's nobility, for his father's strength and influence?

"Blessed are they that hunger." Bless God! What are we hungering for a little bit of God, enough to take us through this old world where we will have the dry rot and be stunted and then squeeze into heaven? "Blessed are they that hunger" for the nature and power and love and understanding of God. Why? They shall be filled.

Not long ago I stood before great audiences of the Churchmen of the world. They said, "Through all your ministry there is one note. It is the call for power." They said, "Do you not think it would be better if the Church was calling for holiness instead of power?" And I replied, "She will never obtain the one without the other. There is something larger than holiness. It is the nature of God." The nature of God has many sides. From every angle that the soul approaches God it reveals a new and different manifestation of Him: love, beauty, tenderness, healing, power, might, wisdom, and so on.

So the Christian who hungers and hungers, bless God, and lifts his soul to God brings God down to meet his own cry. The spirit of man and the Spirit of God unite. The nature of God is reproduced in man as God purposed it should be. There are no sick folk in God. There is no sickness in His nature.

There is an incident in the life of Jesus that is so marvelous. Jesus Christ demanded His right to heal a woman who was bound by Satan with a spirit of infirmity, and He was not satisfied until it was accomplished. Devil and Church and creed and preacher went down before the call of the Son of God to assert His right to deliver that soul from sin and sickness. "Blessed are they that hunger."

18

THE STRONG MAN'S WAY TO GOD

Musicians talk of an ultimate note. That is a note you will not find on any keyboards. It is a peculiar note. A man sits down to tune a piano, or any fine instrument. He has no guide to the proper key, and yet he has a guide. That guide is the note that he has in his soul. And the nearer he can bring his instrument into harmony with that note in his soul, the nearer perfection he has attained.

There is an ultimate note in the heart of the Christian. It is the note of conscious victory through Jesus Christ. The nearer our life is tuned to that note of conscious victory; the greater the victory that will be evidenced in our life.

In my ministry in South Africa there was a young lady, one of the most beautiful souls I have ever known. She was baptized in the Spirit when perhaps only seventeen or eighteen years old. One of the remarkable developments in her after her baptism in the Spirit was, that the Spirit of God would come powerfully upon her on occasions, and at such times she would sit down at the piano and translate the music her soul heard. Other times the Spirit would come upon her so powerfully that she would be caused to sing the heavenly music in some angelic language.

God gave her the gift of interpretation, so that quite frequently when the Spirit would come upon her, she would re-sing the song in English, or Dutch as the case might be. Her father and mother were both musicians. They soon learned that when the Spirit thus came upon her, they could record the music. The father would stand at one side and take the words of the song as she sang them, while the mother stood at the other side and recorded the music as she played the music on the instrument. In this way a great deal of the music was preserved.

Some years later, Clara Butts, the great prima donna came to Africa. She was singing at the Wanderers Hall in Johannesburg. One evening after the concert, while being entertained at the hotel, I was introduced to her. She said to me, "Mr. Lake, I have been very anxious to meet you, for I have heard that among your people is a remarkable woman who receives music in the Spirit, apparently of a different realm than ours." I said, "Yes, that is a fact." She inquired if it would be possible to meet her and so a meeting was arranged.

One evening, we went to her hotel, and as we sat down, Clara Butts said to the young lady, "I wish you would sit down and play some of the music I have heard about." She did not understand that such music only came at such times as the Spirit came powerfully upon the woman. However, the young lady sat down at the piano. I said to the company, "Let us bow our heads in prayer." As we did and waited, presently the Spirit of God descended upon her, and then there poured through her soul some of that wondrous, beautiful, heavenly music. I waited to note the affect on the company. When the song was finished, I looked especially at Clara Butts, who was weeping silently. She arose to her feet, and coming forward to the piano she reached out her hands, saying, "Young lady. That music belongs to a world that my soul knows little about. I pray every day of my life God may permit me to enter. In that realm is the ultimate which my soul sometimes hears, but which I have never been able to touch myself."

Beloved, in the Christian life, in the heart of God, there is an ultimate note. That note which is so fine and sweet and true and pure and good that it causes all our nature to respond to it, and rejoices the soul with a joy unspeakable.

All down through the ages some have touched God and heard that ultimate note. I believe that as David sat on the mountainside as a boy, caring for his father's sheep, God by the Spirit taught him the power and blessing of that ultimate note., I believe at times that his soul ascended into God so that many of the Psalms of David are the real soul note of that blessed expression of heavenly music and heaven consciousness which came into the soul of the shepherd boy.

Mary, the Mother of Jesus, understood that note. I remember when I was a young man in a Methodist

Bible Class, which I taught, we were discussing the subject of the Magnificat, that glorified expression which burst from the soul of Mary as she met Elizabeth, when the Spirit came upon her and revealed to her friend that she was to be the Mother of Jesus. In our worldly wisdom we decided of course that the Jewish women of necessity must have been educated to compose that character of poetry spontaneously.

Many a day afterward as I saw the Spirit of God descend upon a soul, and the soul break forth into a song of God, the song of the angels, in a note so high and sweet and pure and clear as no human voice ever had produced perhaps without it, I understood the marvel that was taking place in the soul of Mary when she broke forth into the heavenly expression of that holy song.

"My soul doth magnify the Lord, and my spirit hath rejoiced in God my Savior," and so on.

It was the Spirit of the Lord. Her spirit had ascended, bless God, into the heavenlies. Her spirit had touched heaven's note. Her spirit was receiving and reproducing the song of joy that she heard, possibly of the angels, or perhaps intuitively from the heart of God.

There is a Christianity, that has that high note in it, bless God. Indeed, Christianity in itself, real Christianity is in that high note of God, that thing of heaven, that is not of earth and is not natural. Bless God, it is more than natural. It is the note of heaven.

It comes to the earth. It fills the soul of man. Man's soul rises into heaven to touch God, and in touching God receives that glorified expression and experience into his own soul, and it is reproduced in his own life and nature.

Beloved, there is a victory in God, the victory that characterizes the common walk of a high born Christian. It is the strong man's salvation. It is the salvation that comes from God because of the fact that the spirit of man touches the Spirit of God and receives that experience that we commonly speak of as the blessing of salvation from God.

But Beloved, the soul that receives from God into their spirit that heavenly touch, knows, bless God, he does not have to be told by man, he knows by the Spirit of God that he has become the possessor of the consciousness of union with the Spirit of God which has enlightened his heart, filled his soul with holy joy, and caused his very being to radiate with God's glory and presence.

The hunger of my soul for many a long day has been that I might be able to so present that high true note of God, that the souls of men would rise up in God to that place of power, purity, and strength where the presence and character and works of Christ are evidenced in and through them. There can be no distinction between the exercise of the real power of God as seen in Jesus and its reproduction in a Christian soul. There is a purity, the purity of heaven, so high, so holy, so pure, so sweet that it makes the life of the possessor radiant with the glory and praise of God.

During one of the periods of extreme necessity in our great work in South Africa, our finances became cut off for various reasons. I was anxious that there should be no letting down of the work we were then doing, and was trusting that it would not be necessary to withdraw our men, who had labored and suffered to get the work established on the frontier.

However, not being able to supply funds to those on the front, I deemed it the only wise thing to do to get them all together in a general conference, and decide what was to be our future action. By great sacrifice, a sacrifice too great for me to tell you of this afternoon, we succeeded in bringing in our missionaries from the front for a council. I told them the existing conditions and we sat down in the night time to decide what would be our future policy. After a time I was invited by a committee to leave the room for a minute or two. While I was in the vestry the brethren in the body of the tabernacle continued their conference and went on discussing the general question. When I returned, they said to me, "Brother Lake, we have arrived at a decision." Old Father Van de Wall spoke for the company. He said, "We have reached this conclusion. There is to be no withdrawal of any man from any position. We feel that the time has come when your soul ought to be relieved of responsibility for us. We feel we have weighted your life long enough, but now by the grace of God we return to our stations to carry on our work. We live or die depending on God. If our wives die, they die, if our families die, they die, if we survive we survive, but we are going back to our stations. This work will never be withdrawn. We have one request. Come and serve the communion of the Lord's Supper to us once more while we stand together."

And as I took the cup they arose and stood in a large circle. I took the bread and passed it. It went from hand to hand around the circle. When it came time to pass the wine I took the cup in my hand, and with the usual statement that Jesus gave in the committal of Himself to God, "My blood in the New Testament," I passed it on, and the next one, looking up to God, he said too, "My blood in the New Testament." And so it passed from hand to hand clear around the circle.

Within a few months I was compelled to bury twelve out of that company. Every one of them might have lived if we could have supplied the ordinary essential things they ought to have received. But beloved, we had made our pledge to God. We had declared by the love of God in our souls, and because of what Christ had done for us, that we would be true to Him, and that in the Name of Christ His gospel should be spread abroad as far as it was in our power to do.

Men have said that the Cross of Christ was not a heroic thing, but I want to tell you that the Cross of Jesus Christ has put more heroism in the souls of men than any other event in human history. Men have lived and rejoiced, and died, believing in the living God, in the Christ of God whose blood cleansed their hearts from sin, and who realized the real high spirit of His holy sacrifice, bless God. They manifested to mankind that same measure of sacrifice, and endured all that human beings could endure, and when endurance was no longer possible they passed on to be with God, leaving the world blessed through the evidence of a consecration deep and true and pure and good, like the Son of God Himself.

We see the note that was in the soul of Paul, and which characterized his message, when he made the splendid declaration which I read from Romans 1:16;

"I am not ashamed of the gospel of Christ; for it is the power of God unto salvation to every one that believeth; to the Jew first, and also to the Greek."

You see the note that touched the souls of men, the note that rang down through the centuries, and which rings in your heart and mine today. Christianity NEVER WAS DESIGNED BY GOD TO MAKE A LOT OF WEAKLINGS. It was designed to bring forth a race of men who were bold and strong and pure and good, blessed be God. The greatest and the strongest and the noblest is always the humblest.

The beautiful thing in the gospel is that it eliminates from the life of man that which is of himself and is natural and fleshly and earthly, bless God. It brings forth the beauteous things within the soul of man, the unselfishness, the life of purity, the peace, the strength and the power of the Son of God. How beautiful it is to have the privilege of looking into the face of one whose nature has been thus refined by the Spirit of the living God within. How beautiful it is when we look into the soul of one whom we realize God has purged by the blood of Christ until the very characteristics of the life and attitudes of the mind of Christ are manifest and evident in him to the glory of God.

Christianity is a strong man's gospel. Christianity, by the grace of God, is calculated to take the weak and fallen and erring and suffering and dying, and by applying the grace and power of God, through the soul of man, to the need of the individual, lift then up to the "Lamb of God which taketh away the sin of the world." Blessed be God.

"Down in the human heart,
Crushed by the tempter,
Feelings lie buried
That grace can restore,
Touched by a loving heart,
Wakened by kindness,
Chords that were broken
Will vibrate once more."

I care not how crushed the soul, how bestialized

the nature, I care not how sensual, if touched by the Spirit of the living God, he will shed off that which is earthly and sensual, and give forth once again the pure note of the living God, heaven's high message, heaven's triumphant song, heaven's high note of living praise to the living God. Blessed be His Name.

God is endeavoring by His Spirit in these days to exalt the souls of men into that high place, that holy life, that heavenly state whereby men walk day by day, hour by hour in the heavenly consciousness of the presence of Christ in the heart of man all the time.

And the presence of Christ in the souls of men can only produce, first the purity that is in Him. For the "Wisdom that cometh from above is first pure," bless God. Purity is of God. Purity is of the nature of Christ. Purity is heaven's highborn instinct, filling the soul of man, making him in His nature, like the Son of God. Upon that purified soul there comes from God that blessed measure of the Holy Spirit, not only purifying the nature, but empowering him by the Spirit so that the activities of God, the gift of His mind, the power of His Spirit is evident by the grace of God in that man's soul, in that man's life, lifting him by the grace of God into that place of holy and heavenly dominion in the consciousness of which Jesus lived and moved and accomplished the will of God always. Not the earth-consciousness, born of the earth and earthy, but the Heaven-consciousness, that high consciousness, that holy consciousness, the consciousness of the living God, of His union with

Him, which caused the Christ to walk as a Prince indeed. Bless God.

He was not bowed and overcome by conditions and circumstances about Him, but realized that the soul of man was a creative power, that it was within his soul, and common to his nature, and the nature of every other man, to protect, accumulate and possess, as sons of God; that through the creative faculty of His soul, the desires of his heart might be brought to pass. Blessed be His Name.

That is the reason God dared to talk as He did to Moses. That is the reason God dared to rebuke a man when he stopped to pray. That is the reason God said, "Why standst thou here and criest unto me? Lift up the rod that is in thy hand, and divide the waters."

Beloved, your soul will never demonstrate the power of God in any appreciable degree until your soul conceives and understands the real vision of the Christ of God, whereby He knew that through His union with the living God His soul became the creative power through which He took possession of the power of God and applied it to the needs of his own soul, and the needs of other lives.

"I am the resurrection and the life," bless God. Lazarus was dead. The friends were weeping, but the Christ was there, Bless God. Opening His soul to God in a cry of prayer the Spirit of God so moved within him that the consciousness of his high dominion in God so possessed Him, that He gave forth that wondrous command, "Lazarus, come forth," and the dead obeyed the call, and the spirit that had gone on into the regions of the dead returned again, was joined to the body, and Lazarus was restored by the power of God. Blessed be His Holy Name.

When a boy, I received my religious training in a little Methodist class meeting. I wish there were some old time Methodist class meetings in these modern days, the kind that had the power of God, and the needs of men's souls were met in them; where people could open their hearts and tell of their temptations and their trials and victories and receive council from one who guided the class.

In such a class meeting, and to such a class meeting, I owe a great deal of the development which God has brought forth in my life.

In one of these class meetings one day, as I sat listening to the testimonies, I observed that there was a kind of weakening trend. People were saying, "I am having such a hard time," "I am feeling the temptations of the world so much," and so forth. I was not able at the time to tell people what was the difficulty. I was only a young Christian. But when they got through I observed the old class leader, a grey headed man. He said something like this, "Brethren, the reason we are feeling the temptations so much, the reason there is a lack of the sense of victory, is because we are too far away from the Son of God. Our souls have descended. They are not in the high place where Christ is. Let our souls ascend, and when

227

they ascend into the realm of the Christ, we will have a new note, it will be the note of victory."

Beloved, that is the difficulty with us all. We have come down out of the heavenlies into the natural, and we are trying to live a heavenly life in the natural state, overburdened by the weights and cares of the flesh and life all about us. Bless God, there is deliverance. There is Victory. There is a place in God where the flesh no longer becomes a bondage. Where, by the grace God, every sensuous state of the human nature is brought into subjection to the living God, where Christ reigns in and glorifies the very activities of a man's nature, making him sweet and pure and clean and good and true. Bless His Holy Name.

I call you today, beloved, by the grace of God, to that high life, to that holy walk, to that heavenly atmosphere, to that life in God where the grace and Spirit and power of God permeates your whole being. More, where not only your whole being is in subjection, but it flows from your nature as a holy stream of heavenly life to bless other souls everywhere by the grace of God.

There was a period in my life when God lifted my soul to a wondrous place of divine power. Indeed, I speak it with all conservativeness when I say that I believe God gave me such an anointing of power as has seldom been manifested in modern life. That anointing remained with me for a period of eight months. One of the evidences of the power of God at that period was that God gave me such a consciousness of dominion to cast out evil spirits that the insane were brought from all quarters of the land, slobbering idiots. In many instances as I approached them, the Spirit of Christ would rise up in me in such dominion that when I got to them I could take hold of them, and looking into their face, would realize that God had given me power to cast it out. Hundreds of times the insane were healed instantly right on the spot.

I have been a student all my life. Not just a student of letters, but of the things of the soul. God helped me by His grace to take note of and analyze the conditions of my own soul. I noted that when that high consciousness of heavenly dominion rested upon my life, there was one thing that stood uppermost in all my consciousness. That was the vision of the triumphant Christ, the Son of God, as pictured by John in the first chapter of Revelation, where He stands forth in the mighty dignity of an overcomer, declaring, "I am He that liveth and was dead, and behold, I am alive forevermore. Amen; and have the keys of hell and of death."

Beloved, I want to tell you that the soul joined to Christ and who exercises the power of God, ascends into that high consciousness of heavenly dominion as it is in the heart of Jesus Christ today, for He is the overcomer, the only Overcomer. But yet, when my soul is joined to His soul, when His Spirit flows like a heavenly stream through my spirit, when my whole nature is infilled and inspired by the life from God, I too, being joined with Him, become an overcomer, in deed and in truth. Glory be to God.

I am glad that God has permitted man, even at intervals to rise into that place of high dominion in God, for it demonstrates the purpose of God. It demonstrates that He purposes we should not only rise into the high place at intervals, but that this should be the normal life of the Christian who is joined to God every day and all the time.

Christianity is not a thing to be apologized for. Christianity was the living conscious life and power of the living God, transmitted into the nature of man until, bless God, man's nature is transformed by the living touch, and the very spirit, soul and being is energized and filled by His life. Thus you become indeed, as Christ intended, a veritable Christ.

That startles some people. But the ultimate of the gospel of Jesus Christ and the ultimate of the redemption of the Son of God, is to reproduce and make every man who is bound by sin and held by sensuousness and enslaved by the flesh, like Himself in deed and in truth, sons of God. Not sons of God on a lower order, but sons of God as Jesus was.

Paul declares, "He gave some apostles, some prophets, some evangelists and some pastors and some teachers." What for? "Till we ALL come into the likeness of the measure of the stature of the fullness of Christ." Bless God. Not a limited life, but an unlimited life. The idea of Christ, the idea of God was that every man, through Jesus Christ, through being joined to Him by the Holy Spirit, should be transformed into Christ's perfect image. Glory be to God. Christ within and Christ without. Christ in your Spirit, Christ in your soul and Christ in your body. Not only living His life, but performing His works by the grace of God, That is the gospel of the Son of God. That is the thing that Paul was not ashamed of. He said, "I am not ashamed of the gospel of Christ, for it is the power of God unto salvation to every one that believeth. To the Jew first, and also to the Greek."

If any man has a question within his soul of the reality of the Baptism of the Holy Spirit as it has been poured out upon the world in these last ten years, that question ought to be settled in your soul forever by one common test. That test is, that it has raised the consciousness of Christianity to realize what real Christianity is.

If anyone wants to analyze the development that has come into Christian consciousness during the last two hundred years, all they have to do is to begin and follow the preaching of the great evangelists who have moved the world. Think of Jonathan Edwards, who thundered the terrors of God and what hell was like until men grasped their seats and, hung on to them, fearing, they were falling into hell itself. Men were moved by FEAR to escape damnation. That was believed to be Christianity. Any coward wanted to keep out of hell. He might not have had one idea in his soul of what was the real true earmark of Christianity.

After a while others went a step further, and you can note the ascending consciousness. They said, "No, saving yourself from hell and punishment is not the ideal of the gospel. The ideal is to get saved so as to go to heaven." And so men were saved in order to get to heaven when they died. I have always had a feeling in my soul of wanting to weep when I hear men pleading with others to become Christians so they will go up to heaven when they die. My God, is there no appeal outside of something absolutely selfish.

Beloved, don't you see that Christianity was unselfishness itself. It had no consideration for the selfish individual. The thing held up above everything else in the world, and the only ideal worthy of a Christian was that you and I and He Himself might demonstrate to mankind one holy, high beauteous thing, of which the world was deficient, and that was a knowledge of God. So Jesus said, "Unto all righteousness" and He wrote it on the souls of men and branded it on their conscience, and stamped it on their heart until the world began to realize the ideal that was in the soul of Jesus.

"Unto all righteousness" becoming like Christ Himself, a demonstration of the righteousness of the living God. That is Christianity, and that only is Christianity, for that was the consecration of the Christ Himself.

The test of the Spirit, and the only test of the Spirit, that Jesus ever gave, is the ultimate and final test. He said, "By their fruits ye shall know them." That is the absolute and final test. "Do men gather grapes of thorns, or figs of thistles?"

So I say to you, if you want to test whether this present, outpouring of the Spirit of God is the real thing, the real pure Baptism of the Holy Ghost or not, test it by the fruit that it produces. If it is producing in the world, as we believe it is, a consciousness of God so high, so pure, so acceptable, so true, so good, so like Christ, then it is the Holy Ghost Himself. Bless God. No other test is of any value whatsoever.

I want to tell you beloved that the ultimate test to your own of the value of a thing that you have in you heart is the common test that Jesus gave, "By their fruits ye shall know them." "By their FRUITS ye shall know them. Do men gather grapes of thorns, or figs of thistles?"

Men tell us in these days that SIN is what you think it is. Well, it is not. Sin is what God thinks it is. You may think, according to your own conscience; God thinks according to His. God thinks in accordance with the heavenly purity of His own nature. Man thinks in accordance with that degree of purity that his soul realizes. But the ultimate note is in God. The finality is in God.

When men rise up in their souls' aspirations to the place of God's thought, then bless God, the character of Jesus Christ will be evident in their life, the sweetness of His nature, the Holiness of His character, the beauty of the crowning glory that not only overshadowed Him, but that radiated from Him. Blessed be God. And the real life of the real Christian is the inner life, the life of the soul.

"Out of the heart," said Jesus, "proceedeth evil thoughts, fornications, adulteries" and so forth. These are the things common to the flesh of man. Out of the soul of man, likewise, proceeds by the same common law, the beauty, virtue, peace, power and truth of Jesus, as the soul knows it.

So he whose soul is joined to Christ may now, today, this hour, shed forth as a benediction upon the world the glory and blessing and peace and power of God, even as Jesus shed it forth to all men to the praise of God.

(Prayer) My God, we bless Thee for the ideal of the gospel of Christ which Thou hast established in the souls of men through the blessed Holy Ghost. God, we pray Thee this afternoon that if we have thought lightly of the Spirit of God, if we have had our eyes fixed on outward evidences instead of the inward life, we pray thee to sweep it away from our souls.

May we this day God, see indeed that the life of God, His inner life, the true life, God's holy life, His practical purpose, that from a race of sinful men saved through the blood of Christ, cleansed by the power of God, cleansed in the inner soul, in every department of their nature, that the Christ-life is to be revealed and the Lord Jesus through them is to shed forth His glory and life and benediction and peace and power upon the world. Blessed be Thy precious Name.

So my God, we open our nature to heaven today, asking that the Spirit of the living God will thus move in our own soul, that by His grace we shall be so perfectly, truly cleansed of God that our nature will be sweet and pure and heavenly and true, so that we can receive from God indeed the blessed sweetness of His pure, holy, heavenly Spirit, to reign in us, to rule in us, control us and guide us for ever more. In Jesus' Name. Amen.

OUR REPLY TO ALL CRITICS AND
INQUIRERS AT MASONIC TEMPLE,
SUNDAY, JUNE 23, 1918

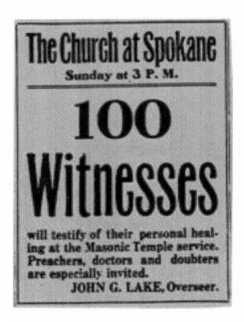

The above was printed in Spokesman Review.
Lake invited all "preachers, doctors, and doubters" to
come and see the healing power of God at work.
What follows is a portion of the article printed in the
same newspaper following their service, publicly
testifying of the glory and goodness of God.

We Promised to Present 100 Cases of Healing on Sunday Last. 267 Persons Testified by Standing, to Having Been Healed by the Power of God. 32 Persons Gave Public Oral Testimony to the Following Miraculous Cures.

Rev. T. Armstrong, a Methodist minister of N2918 Columbus avenue, healed of a sarcoma growing out of the left shoulder three times as large as a human head.

Rev. Thomas B. O'Riley, 430 Rookery building, healed of fits so violent that it required seven policemen to overpower and confine him in the hospital. Instantaneous healing.

Baby Agnes Young, N169 Post street. Patient at Deaconess hospital for six months for malnutrition; weighted six pounds at birth, at 9 months weighed five pounds. Was removed from hospital; ministered to in prayer; perfectly well in six weeks.

Mrs. Chittenden, Truth church, Coeur d'Alene, Idaho, healed of cancers of the breast.

Mrs. Everetts, 1911 Boone avenue—Varicose veins; suffered for 38 years; veins enlarged the size of a goose egg; is perfectly healed.

Mrs. Constance Hoag, Puyallup, Wash.—Broke her kneecap and bone protruded through the flesh. Applied an anointed handkerchief. Was perfectly healed in an hour. Knee just as well as the other.

Mrs. Walker, Granby Court—Incurable internal

cancer; severe case of neuritis; healed through prayer.

Mrs. Harriet Petersen, 2815 Illinois avenue—Was operated on and organs removed. Operated on the second time for gallstones. Bad recovery. Perfectly healed when in a state of death. Is now a healthy, normal woman.

Asa Hill, Palouse, Wash.—Rheumatic cripple for 15 years; instantly healed, now works his farm.

Mrs. Wolferman—Injured in G. N. R. R. wreck. Awarded large damages by court. (see court record.) Physicians testified her injuries were such that they destroyed the possibility of motherhood. Healed in answer to prayer. Gave birth to a son at Dr. William T. Penn's private hospital.

Miss Pearl Payne, E827 Rockwell—Came to Spokane to die. Disease, diabetes, healed, and is working every day.

Miss Jennie Walsh, Union Park, S116 Fiske street —Gallbladder filled with pus. Physicians insisted on immediate operation. Was instantly healed through prayer.

Mr. Flieshman, Leland, Idaho—Kidney was filled with pus. Physicians said kidney must be removed to save his life. Ministered to and healed when hands were laid upon him.

Mrs. Lamphear, 115 1-2 Sprague avenue—Invalid 11 years. Prolapsus of stomach, bowels of stomach and uterus. Tuberculosis and rheumatism. While taking treatments at Soap Lake her left leg grew three inches longer than the other and her foot one inch too long. A bone as large as an orange developed on inside of left knee. Was ministered to at healing rooms. Tubercular lungs healed, leg shortened at the rate of an inch a week, and the bone growth on knee disappeared. Limbs are of equal length. She is perfectly well.

Miss Adelia Koch, 1115 First avenue— Pronounced incurable by 73 physicians (regulars). Later was taken to osteopathic institute at Los Angeles. Was a patient there three and a half years. Returned to Spokane in the same dying condition. Had been operated on 26 times. Her father testifies that the doctors got his three houses in Davenport, a valuable wheat ranch of 160 acres, 147 carloads of wood, and all the money he had. Is healed and earning her own living.

Mrs. Carter, wife of Policeman Carter, W31 Pacific avenue—Was examined by seven physicians who pronounced her condition due to a large fibroid tumor which they estimated would weigh 15 pounds. Was perfectly healed in four ministrations at the healing rooms.

Mrs. O. D. Stutzman, Hansen apartments—Invalid 13 years. Lay in Sacred Heart hospital with a 20-pound weight attached to her foot for 32 days while suffering with inflammatory rheumatism. Begged to be taken home. Preferred to be a cripple rather than endure the torture any longer. Was instantly healed when Mr. Lake laid his hands upon her and prayed.

Mr. John De Witt of Granby Court—Testified on

behalf of his friend, Mr. Fred Narnard, who is 32 years of age. Was injured in babyhood, caused curvature of spine. Was perfectly healed at healing rooms in six days. Height increased one inch. Passed army medical examination and is now in England with troops.

Mr. and Mrs. Harry Lotz stand holding their baby in their arms. Baby developed pus in kidneys and was pronounced incurable by physicians. Instantly healed in answer to prayer.

God in Surgery.

Mrs. Gilbertson, N4115 Helena Street—Hip came out of joint through disease and would turn like the leg of a doll, showing it was entirely out of socket. Was prayed for at the healing rooms while she was suffering in her home, four miles across the city. As prayer was offered the power of God came upon her and the joint was perfectly set.

Remarks by Rev. Lake when testimony was given: "Do you hear it, you folks who worship a dead Christ? You doctors, hear it? You preachers, hear it? You doubters, hear it? God set the woman's hip. Because faith in God applied the blessed power to her life."

One of the most remarkable cases in history— The Risdon family stand holding their 6-year-old son on their shoulders. This boy was born with a closed head. In consequence the skull was formed upward like the gable of a house, also the forehead was the same. Through the pressure on the brain the right side became paralyzed and the child could not speak. Under divine healing ministration the bones softened and spread out, the shape of the head became perfectly normal and the paralysis disappeared and he received the power of speech.

Remarks by Rev. Lake—"I want you to see that in the spirit of God there is a science far beyond what is termed science and the man or woman who enters into spirit relation with God and exercises. His power is most scientific."

Mr. Allen, pastor of Pentecostal mission, was dying of pellagra. Was carried from the train into the baggage room as dead. Was instantly healed through the laying on of hands and prayer.

Mrs. Lena Lakey, W116Riverside avenue— Instantly healed of violent insanity. An abscess in her left side, from which she had suffered for 15 years, disappeared in 24 hours. A heavy rheumatic bone deposit between the bones of the fingers and the joints of the toes disappeared in 48 hours. She is perfectly well.

Mrs. Holder—Healed of insanity while at Medical Lake institution.

At this point, the newspaper from the archives is damaged and mostly unreadable, but many more testimonies followed, to include people healed from stomach cancer, drunkenness, neuritis, and swollen

legs. As this is a list of testimonies of God's healing power, the editor saw fit to include what was available rather than nothing at all. We hope that you agree.

20

COLLECTED LETTERS, ARTICLES, AND MISCELLANEA

A Call For Helpers

Printed in The Pentecost, Indianapolis, Indiana, December, 1908

Johannesburg, Transvaal.

DEAR SISTER SMOCK—

I want to make this letter strictly business. I know your soul is wrapped up in missionary work, so is mine. I want you to realize in some degree what I can only tell you that Johannesburg is unquestionably the greatest field for missionary work in the known world. In the last three or four years the natives from the very interior of Africa have been coming up to Johannesburg to work on the mines. They live in the compounds and on any Sunday forenoon YOU CAN ADDRESS 2,500 NATIVES in most of the compounds.

About 150 mines are in operation, each of which employs from 1,000 to 3,000 natives who are accommodated in compounds, buildings built in a square with a court in the center, where an additional building is placed as a kitchen. These compounds are scattered along the railroad at the various mines for fifty miles.

The thing that my heart is on is this, that some of these souls who have been waiting and preparing and praying and praying, and apparently getting nowhere, get into God's order of getting things from Him and come as God has called them, and commence to use the faith they have got, and as they use it they will get more.

Oh, beloved, God is doing a wonderful work here. I cannot tell you what wonderful manifestations of the Spirit of God that we see every day, in depth of character a hundred times beyond anything I have ever seen anywhere. But there is such a demand for workers at this time. I could place a hundred workers today if they were only here.

Sister Smock, in Jesus' name do get a hold of some of the home people and get them into clearer light and real faith in God and believe Him for coming here. There are FIFTY THOUSAND CHINESE HERE. They live in compounds too. The Chinese Missionary from Canton who ministers to them was baptized with the Holy Ghost at one of our cottage meetings a week ago last night. He is a precious fellow. One of the Baker Missionaries, Bro. Ingram, has received his baptism. A Dutch Missionary next door to where we live, Mr. van Marile, has received his baptism.

The Congregational Church at Pretoria, after observing the healings there, has commenced to pray for the sick, and one young man in the last stages of consumption was healed in answer to their prayers. One of the Baker missions has commenced to pray for the sick. Two sick natives were brought to their meetings and were instantly healed and praised God in a wonderful way.

I do have it in my soul that GOD WANTS TO USE YOU in America as a recruiting officer and to take up some of these people who have calls and get them out here. These people that are wondering about where they are called to, if they have got a call anywhere, God can use them here. There are not only hundreds of thousands of natives, and Chinamen, but there are thousands of Mohammedans and natives of India all over Africa. If they have got a call to India, this is India enough. If they have a call to China, this is China enough. But dear Sister Smock, one thing that I can be assured of, you will not encourage anyone of doubtful or insincere experience to come.

Your brother in Christ,

John G. Lake

The Secret of Power

Given in tongues by the Holy Ghost to John G. Lake, at 2 a.m. June 18th, 1910. Cookhouse C. C. South Africa

(Luke 24:49 and Acts 1:8)

He is risen, He is risen! Hear the cry
Ringing through the land, and sea and sky.
'Tis the shout of victory, triumph is proclaimed
Heralds of God announce it, Death's disdained.

Shout the tidings! Shout the tidings! Raise the cry.
Christ's victorious, Christ's victorious can not die,
For the bars of death He sundered, Satan sees that he
    has blundered,
As the shouts of angels thundered, "He's alive!"

Catch the shout, ye earth-born mortals, let it roll,
Till it echoes o'er the mountains from the center to
    the poles
That the Christ of earth and Glory death has
    conquered.
Tell the story, He's the Victor! He's the Victor! So
    am I.

For this reason that my ransom He has paid,
I've accepted His atonement on Him laid,
He, the Lamb of God that suffered all for me,
Bore my sins, my griefs, my sickness on the tree.

I am risen, I am risen from the grave,
Of my sins, my griefs, my sickness, and the waves
Of the resurrection life, and holy power
Thrill my being with His new life every hour.

Now the lightnings of God's Spirit burn my soul,
Flames of His divine compassion o'er me roll,
Lightning power of God's own Spirit strikes the
   power of hell.
God in man, Oh Glory! Glory! all the story tell.

I have proved Him, I have proved Him. It is true,
Christ's dominion yet remaineth, 'tis for you,
Let the fires of holy passion sweep your soul.
Let the Christ who death has conquered take control.
He will use you, He will use you. Zion yet has
   Saviors still,
Christ the Conqueror only waiteth for the action of
   your will.

Sanctification and Holy Living

Printed in The Pentecost, June, 1909

I have seen that there is much confusion and
apparent misconception of the teaching of
sanctification and the teaching of holy living as taught
by some of the advanced teachers. I feel compelled to
write a short article calling attention to the actual
difference in this teaching, believing that it may be a
blessing to others who have tried to live a holy life
and really practice holy living to the best of their
ability and have been unable to satisfy their own
hearts that their present experience is in the will of
God. Salvation, healing and holy living has been the
standard of Christian teaching among many, and

many have struggled to live a holy life who have found it impossible to be holy according the the Bible standard and their own conscience. This article is written in the hope that these may be able to see and enter into the real inwrought experience of a real sanctified life in God; that will make it possible for them to live a holy life.

Holy living as taught among modern Christian teachers has meant that in our outward every day living we shall imitate the life of Christ; that we shall be clean men and clean women; that the purity of our life shall be unquestionable; that in all our acts we shall act like Christ.

This is really Christian Ethics and is not scriptural holiness.

Holiness of heart and ethics are very closely connected. They correlate and interact. Their right adjustment and mutual development is the problem before us.

At one time in the world's history ethics was exalted above inward experience as though purity of heart was caused by holy living. This has been the great error. At another time inward experience was exalted above ethics as though purity of heart existed independent of holy living. For two hundred years the pendulum has swung, first to the one extreme, then to the other. Both of these theories come of limited one-sided views of Christianity; the former obtained before the Wesleyan reformation. Thomas à Kempis in his book, "The Imitation of Christ," was the first great teacher of holy living. Excepting the Bible, this book is declared to have been translated more often and more widely read than any other book. It is said to have reached five hundred editions. This book was published in the latter half of the Fourteenth century. In 1650, Bishop Jeremy Taylor published his "Holy Living and Dying." This followed in the line of "The Imitation of Christ."

Following Jeremy Taylor's "Holy Living and Dying," seventy-five years later, came William Law's "Serious Call to a Devout and Holy Life," and his "Practical Treatise Upon Christian Perfection."

These books are the foundation of the teaching of holy living and are written from the standpoint of Christian ethics. They emphasize purity of heart, but fail to particularize the act of faith by which the heart is cleansed from sin.

"And put no difference between us and them, purifying their hearts by faith" (Acts 15:9).

"To open their eyes, and to turn them from darkness to light, and from the power of Satan into God, that they may receive forgiveness of sins, and inheritance among them which are sanctified by faith that is in me" (Acts 26:18).

Nor God's act of faith by which the heart is instantly cleansed from indwelling.

"Knowing this, that our old man is crucified with him, that the body of sin might be destroyed, that henceforth we should not serve sin" (Romans 6:6).

"For the law of the Spirit of life in Christ Jesus

hath made me free from the law of sin and death" (Romans 8:2).

"And the very God of peace sanctify you wholly; and I pray God your whole spirit and soul and body be preserved blameless unto the coming of our Lord Jesus Christ."

They bent their force upon holy living and this left the impression that purity of heart would result from holy living. Influenced by these books, John and Charles Wesley in 1729 followed after holiness and incited others to do so.

In 1737 they saw likewise that men are justified before they are sanctified (Methodist Discipline, page 13). Here it appears that John Wesley aimed at holy living for eight years before he ever saw that he must be first sanctified by the blood of Jesus before he could be holy either in heart or life. How many of us have made the same error? How many of us have tried and tried to live a holy life with the old nature of sin still in our breast. When the heart is purified from all sin then the outer life will manifest it.

Is it any wonder that people failed when the author of "Holy Living and Dying" did not even profess justification. He says on pages 292-293, "A true penitent must all the days of his life pray for pardon and never think the work completed until he dies... and whether God hath forgiven us of no, we know not." In the face of this teaching, the clear cut teaching of John Wesley on the nature of entire sanctification wrought in an instant by a divine act conditioned alone upon a specific act of sanctifying faith in the Blood of Christ, followed by endless growth in holiness of heart and life, stands forth in marvelous grandeur. In fact, for putting the clear evenly balanced, well-rounded, all-including, ever-abounding scriptural holiness, John Wesley has no equal. With him as with us, holiness was "having the mind of Christ" and walking as Christ also walked, even having not some part only but all the mind which was in him and walking as he walked, not only in many or most respects, but in all things, so that the purpose of God is really made a fact in our lives (see Ephesians 1:4). "According as he hath chosen us in him before the foundation of the world that we should be holy and without blame before him in love." "And you, that were sometime alienated and enemies in your mind by wicked works, yet now hath he reconciled in the body of his flesh through death, to present you holy and unblameable and unreproveable in his sight" (Colossians 1:21-22)

Oh, glory! He can do it. He can do it. He has done it for me. Hallelujah! Hallelujah!

Asleep in Jesus

Printed in The Pentecost, Indianapolis, Indiana, January, 1909

Just as we are going to press we are in receipt of a letter from Bro. John G. Lake, 4 Millbourn Rd., Bertram, Johannesburg, South Africa, one of the party of missionaries who left Indianapolis last April for missionary work in South Africa, that his wife has been called home to be with Jesus. While we feel the loss of our dear sister deeply, and especially does our heart go out for Bro. Lake as he is left alone to wage this Christian warfare, yet we are glad that we shall see her again on that glorious day when this corruption shall put on incorruption and we shall arise together with those who are now asleep to Him to be forever with the Lord. Bro, Lake's letter follows:

My dear Bro. Flower and all the dear friends in America:

I write to tell you that my precious wife was called home to heaven, December 22nd, at 9 p.m.

I was absent in the Orange Free State holding native conferences in connection with Bro. Inahon, when I received a telegram from Allie, my oldest son, saying, "Mamma is ill, come." I took the first train but she was dead when I got home. Horace (14) and Johnnie (4) were mixed up in a bicycle accident a month ago and were knocked unconscious for quite a long time. Both recovered, but the shock seemed to take hold of Mrs. Lake so she could not eat properly after I had gone away on my last trip. She wrote me Friday, Dec. 18, saying that she was not very well but urging me to remain until the conference closed and I received a little rest.

That evening she sat on the porch late, took a chill, rheumatic fever developed, and before she or our friends or any one realized she was really ill, it went to her heart and she was dead. She just went to sleep and never woke up here.

Oh! I cannot express what it means to us with our seven babies, but Alexander, my oldest son (16) has been such a strength to me in the trial.

I cannot explain the marvelous way the dear Lord has used Mrs. Lake here. Her spiritual life, that was always deep and clear, seemed to deepen and deepen into God day by day until she seemed for months to be more on the other side than this.

More people have been baptized under her ministry here than any one of the party. As her dear body lay in our home, the people whom God has blessed, saved and healed, and baptized, came in hundreds to offer a last token of love.

One woman, who was blind and healed four weeks ago when Mrs. Lake prayed for her, came to kiss the dear cold hands. Another, the wife of one of the large merchants, who was healed when dying of appendicitis at the Kensington Sanitarium, and many, many more. I mention these cases as they are exceptionally pathetic ones.

I can only go on and trust God. However, I am determined, by God's help, not to permit the children to be scattered. We will maintain our home at all hazards; but oh, beloved, only those who have known our stormy life know the loss that has come to me. In all our battles, whether the devil roared or the world frowned or hissed or fawned at our feet, she was just the same, and while I cannot understand His ways in permitting her to leave my side, my faith is unshaken, my confidence is in Him and I am going forward. But the problems that were large before are larger now.

On Tuesday night, one week before her death, at the close of the cottage meeting at our home, Miss Radford, a missionary from Natal, was baptized and spoke in tongues as Mrs. Lake and she prayed together. It was a great anxiety to her that any member of our household should not be baptized by Jesus with the Holy Ghost. When Miss Radford was baptized, she was the last of those who worked with us in our home work except Pete, the native kitchen boy, a young man of twenty-five years. About four hours before she left us, she sent for Pete to come and pray. As he knelt at her bedside, she put her hands on his head and prayed and Jesus baptized him, and when Miss Radford returned to her bedside, Mrs. Lake and Pete were both speaking and praying in tongues.

The Dutch people here called her "The Missus who Prays." They come inquiring for the "Missus Who Prays" yet. Oh, dear one, do bear me and our family up in your prayers.

I cannot stop. I must go on.

Two months ago, one day as I sat at the desk, she was standing near me. I was looking at the marvelous spirituality of her face when she suddenly turned, and kissing me, said, "Poor Jack, you did not know you brought me to Africa to die, did you?" Then she kissed me quickly and was gone before I realized the import of what it meant.

Though I was hundreds of miles away, I knew, through the spirit, what was transpiring, though I could not reach her.

Her life was a sacrifice for others. During the awful press of this work, when we were worn out for want of sleep, she would come and say, "Now Jack, you go to bed and let me pray with the rest of these people," and though I had no special liberty to leave home the last time, she made the arrangements so that I was practically forced to go. She hoped I would return rested.

Oh I feel that she gave her life for others. Dear ones at Indianapolis, you knew her. You will pray for me I know. Also the other dear friends in America.

Your Brother in Jesus, our coming, conquering King,

John G. Lake.

P.S.—The last vision Jesus gave her was just a short time before she fell into her final sleep. She said to Sister Tim, "Oh, I see a beautiful pure white marble cross." The boys and myself are determined we will have a small white marble cross for her grave. She is buried in Braamfontein Cemetery, Johannesburg, South Africa.

Bro. Tom was absent in Pretoria at the time of her death, also Alexander, Horace and Otto, our oldest sons. She never knew she was going apparently. She never said a word about it to any one. She just fell asleep in Jesus.

Latest News From Africa

Printed in The Pentecost, Indianapolis, Indiana, September, 1908

39 Van Beek St.
Doornfontein, Johnnesburg, S. Africa

God has wonderfully blessed the work here in South Africa. Manifestations of the Spirit have been intense in their power and depth of character beyond anything I have known. Some of the most striking things have occurred. In the meeting at Pretoria two weeks ago two-thirds of the congregation—the entire hall being filled—were prostrate under the power of God at one time, saint and sinner alike. Such confessions of sin, even of crimes, I have never before witnessed.

At one meeting we laid hands on I think not less than forty persons for healing and the baptism. The sick were instantly healed and the power of God came upon them in such a degree that they fell on the floor and lay under the power for hours. The same thing occurred with those for whom we prayed for the baptism. Bro. Lehman and I believe that 75 percent of all the people we have prayed for have been instantly healed.

This morning we were called to pray for a dying

woman given up to die of pneumonia. God instantly healed her, and when I left the house her pain was all gone, her fever had disappeared, and she was perfectly well though weak. It has been so every day. We have been having conversions and sanctifications at every service, and a great many have received their baptism. In fact it is the most wonderful Apostolic Faith work I have yet seen.

The seats in the Zion Tabernacle where we are now conducting services on Sunday evenings are not only filled, but hundreds stand throughout the entire service, and on week nights the seats are filled and usually large numbers have to stand.

I have never before had such messages from the Lord as I have received this week. The message on Wednesday night was the most remarkable the Lord has ever spoken through me. It was a message to the Jews. From 200 to 300 Jews attend every service. The message was from the 22nd Psalm, Zechariah 12:10, see also Zechariah 13:6, Luke 2, and the first chapter of Revelation.

I am conscious that the prayers of the saints at home are being answered in our behalf in a mighty manner. I have but one desire in my soul and that is to do the whole will of God.

Missionaries who have lived here ever since the town commenced to build thirty-three years ago, assure us every day that Johannesburg was never so religiously stirred before. Some of the very hardest men in the city have been saved. In fact many times at night when I come home from the meeting men are waiting at the house to be pointed to the Lord. When I get up in the morning others are there. I have hardly been able to eat, let alone sleep, and the only danger in the whole matter is, that the incessant, constant strain may wear me out physically. It is just the same with Bros. Tom and Lehman.

Praying the blessing of God upon every saint at Indianapolis, and asking that you pray earnestly for me that I shall keep low at Jesus' feet that all His will may be wrought out in me. I am yours till He come.

The Vision

Given to John G. Lake October 10, 1909, in tongues with interpretation.

Jesus thou King! Glorious and eternal!
Mighty and loving! Powerful and grand!
Who through the blackness and darkness infernal
Guideth and holdeth Thy child by the hand.

Pierced is Thy soul! Grieved is Thy Spirit!
Bleeding Thy feet are! Wounded Thy hand!
Sorrowing Christ, through the Veil now uplifted
See I Thy beckoning with uplifted hand.

Hear I Thy voice as to me Thou now speakest!
See I Thy teardrops silently fall!
Know I the anguish Thy sorrowing Spirit
Feels as Thou drinkest this wormwood and gall.

What, Lord, the cause of Thy anguish of Spirit?
Why doth this suffering come to Thee now?
Crucified once, on the cross wast Thou lifted?
Have not the cruel thorns pierced Thy brow?

Have not the sins of mankind on Thee rested
Causing Thy soul in anguish to be torn?
Has not the blood-sweat from Thee been wrested?
Have not Thy saints for the crucified mourned?

Why is it then that again now I see Thee
Bruised and bleeding, anguished and lone?
Why is the Spirit of Christ now within me
Witnessing thus of Thy sorrow again?

List to the answer! Let all the world hear it!
Jesus is speaking! Let all hear His voice!
It is because of the sins of my people.
It is because ye will not heed My voice.

Do ye not bite and devour one another?
Do ye not slay with your tongue and pen?
Many of my precious daughters and mothers,
Young men and maidens, E'en boys and old men?

Have ye e'er stood in the fire where they're tested?
Have ye e'er felt of the withering blast?
Know ye how long and how hard they've resisted
Fighting and struggling unto the last?

Guidance

Given in the Spirit in tongues with interpretation to John G. Lake at Johannesburg, South Africa, 1908.

Oh, Soul, on the highway, from earth unto glory
Surrounded by mysteries, trials and fears;
Let the life of thy God, in thy life be resplendent;
For Jesus will guide thee; thou need'st never fear.

For if thou wilt trust me, I'll lead thee and guide thee
Through the quicksands and deserts of life, all the
    way.
No harm shall befall thee; I only will teach thee
To walk in surrender with Me day by day.

For earth is a school to prepare thee for Glory;
The lessons here learned, you will always obey.
When eternity dawns, it will be only the morning
Of life with Me always, as life is today.

Therefore, be not impatient, as lessons thou'rt
    learning;
Each day will bring gladness and joy to thee here;
But heaven will reveal to thy soul, of the treasure
Which infinitude offers, through ages and years.

For thy God is the God of the earth and heavens;
And thy soul is the soul that He died to save;
And His blood is sufficient, His power eternal;
Therefore rest in thy God, both today and alway.

Thus concludes your book.

But take heart! There is much more reading to do!

This is only one book in a series of Lake's sermons.
We have also carefully collected any recommendations
that he made throughout these sermons,
and have included them all at the following link:

http://JawboneDigital.com/Lake

Made in United States
Orlando, FL
09 October 2023

37721720R00162